D1062308

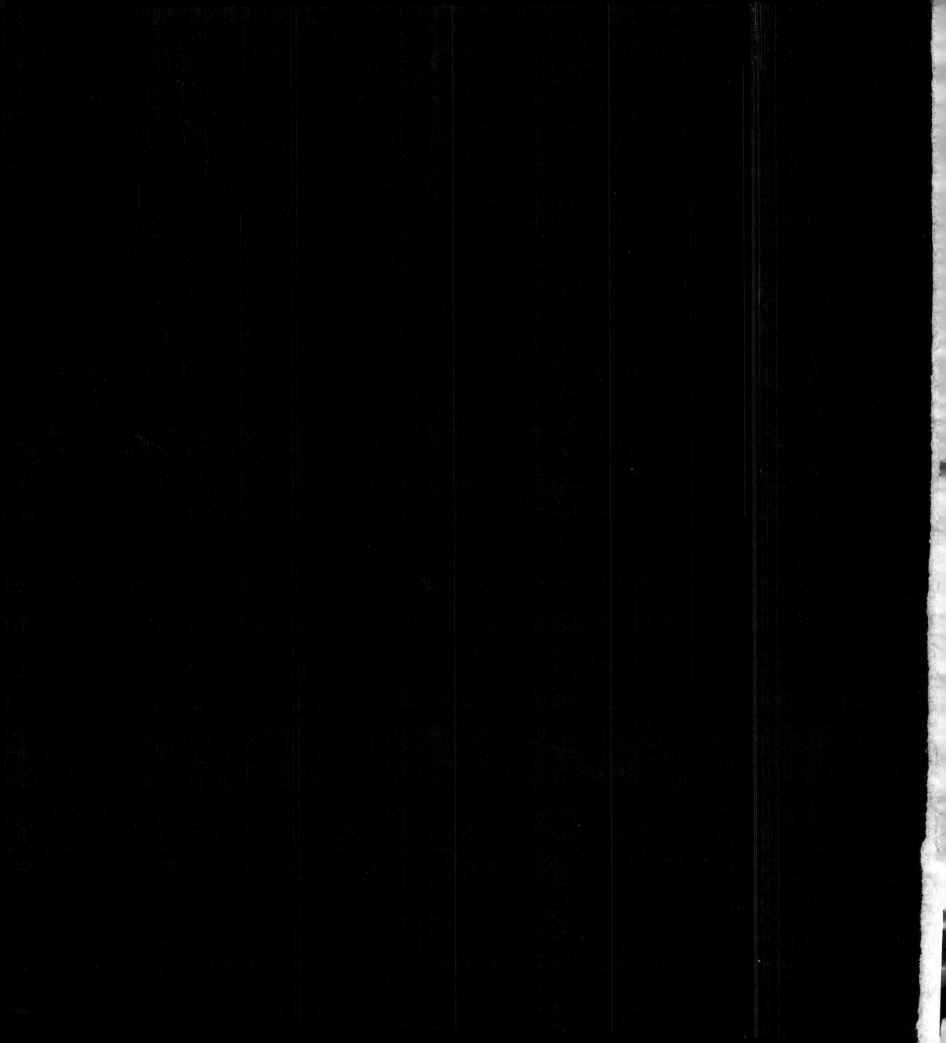

Architecture of the Old South

NORTH CAROLINA

Architecture of the Old South

NORTH CAROLINA

MILLS LANE

Special Photography by VAN JONES MARTIN
Editorial Assistance by MARSHALL BULLOCK
Drawings by GENE CARPENTER

The Beehive Press   SAVANNAH · GEORGIA

Frontispiece: Moravian Church, Salem, 1798–1800.

© The Beehive Press 1985

Library of Congress Catalogue No. 85–071271

Contents

293822

WEST GEORGIA REGIONAL LIBRARY SYSTEM

NORTH CAROLINA

0   10   20   30   40   50

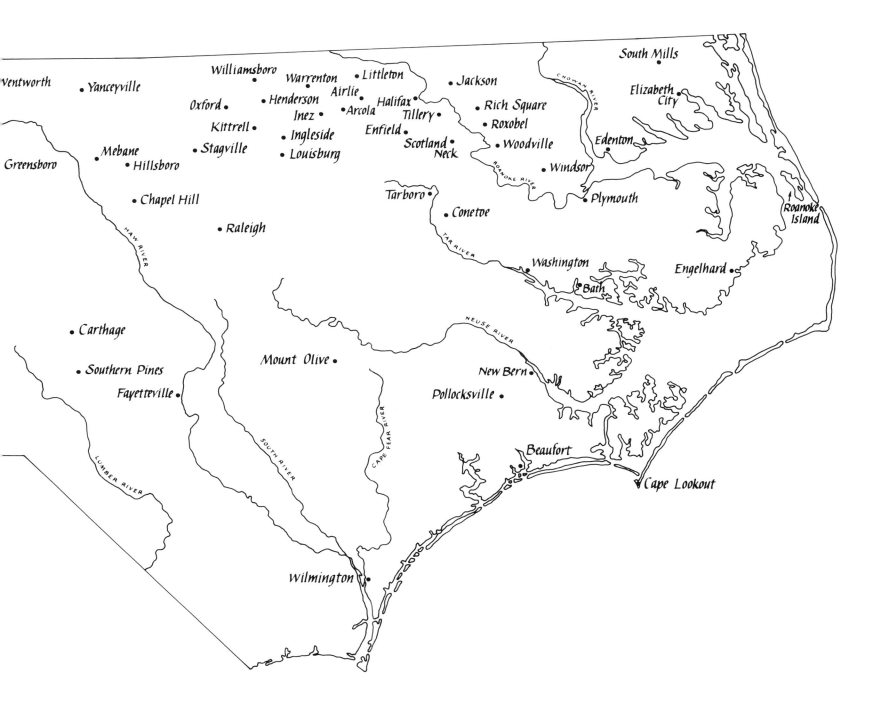

Foreword

This volume continues a series of books about the historic buildings of the Old South. Each volume illustrates and describes the important and beautiful buildings of one or two states in a sensible chronological and stylistic order, all set in a brief cultural and social background but without any attempt to make a dogmatic architectural thesis. Just as every student, including this one, leans on the researches of others, this book is intended as a framework for further study.

There have been many books about American architecture in general but few recent serious ones about particular states. Survey books too often illustrate the same famous buildings, some of which their authors may have never seen in person, and repeat the same observations and some of the same errors, select didactic examples and impose a grand, if artificial, orderliness on the subject. Every serious student knows North Carolina's most famous buildings—Cupola House, the Governor's Palace, the Moravian buildings of Salem and the State Capitol. But how many know Old Brick House, an 18th-century dwelling with fully panelled interiors copied from Batty Langley, or Little Manor, the most sumptuous house of the Federal era in North Carolina, or Cooleemee with its extraordinary cruciform plan and ornament taken from a mid 19th-century pattern book, or some twenty buildings designed by famed A. J. Davis of New York, or Harriet Irwin's eccentric hexagonal houses?

The Civil War represents the triumph of industrialization, homogenizing the nation's cultural life and beginning the end of regionalism in American architecture. But despite this series' title, *Architecture of the Old South*, buildings throughout America were probably more alike than they were different. The great architectural styles of early America—colonial Georgian, Adamesque Federal, the Greek Revival and Gothic Revival—were international movements. The well-to-do people of the South who had a taste for academically stylish buildings were travelled and educated. Many of the greatest buildings of the South were designed by professionals from outside the region or copied from builders' pattern books published at London, Boston, Philadelphia or New York, often used by newcomers from New England, a group whose contributions to life and architecture of the Old South have been generally overlooked. North Carolina's colonial trade was principally carried on by "the merchants and Store Keepers of Virginia and the people of New England." The late 18th-century State House at Raleigh and the early 19th-century Governor's House were built by two different housewrights from Massachusetts.

In addition to the omnipresent influence of people and trade from England and Virginia, the city of Philadelphia seems to have contributed more than any other single place to North Carolina's architecture. In colonial times, ships sailed regularly between Philadelphia and New Bern and Wilmington. John Hawks, architect of the colonial Governor's Palace, was sent to Philadelphia for material and workmen. Settlers from Philadelphia and other parts of Pennsylvania made their way down the Shenandoah Valley of Virginia to the Piedmont of North Carolina in the mid-18th century and continued to send wagons back and forth for hardware, locks and other vital building supplies. Glass for the first State House at Raleigh came from Philadelphia. William Williams, one of the great landowners and tastemakers of the post-Revolutionary period, made two trips to Philadelphia each year. The two most influential architectural books used in North Carolina during the first quarter of the 19th century were Owen Biddle's *Young Carpenter's Assistant*, published at Philadelphia in 1805, and John Haviland's *Builder's Assistant*, published at Philadelphia in 1818. The North Carolina Capitol was built almost completely by artisans from Philadelphia and with cast iron, chimneypieces, chandeliers and other materials from Philadelphia.

Indeed, upon a close look at the architecture of one state, the forces of localism seem stronger than regionalism. The special cultural and economic factors shaping one prosperous community, one influential patron and his admirers or one talented craftsman and his apprentices or imitators often created clusters of buildings with distinctive plans and decorations. In North Carolina, some outstanding local types are the small brick two- and three-room, gambrel-roof houses of the Albemarle with their brick chimney ends and frame front and rear walls, the delightful Palladian-inspired three-part farm houses of the upper counties in the early 19th century, the elegant Federal houses of New Bern with their superbly carved interiors, the exuberant Italianate designs of Jacob Holt in Warren County, or the vivid individuality of A. J. Davis's designs at Chapel Hill, Greensboro, Raleigh and Davidson.

Buildings are three-dimensional history books which reflect the comings and goings, successes and failures of real people. North Carolina's surviving early architecture is modest in scale and small in quantity because the colony, despite an early start, had treacherous coasts, poor harbors and shallow rivers and developed slowly. After the Revolution, the upper counties, enriched by tobacco trade with Virginia, produced North Carolina's finest buildings. Despite the general shifting of population from the older states of the upper South to the fertile new lands of the Mississippi Valley, North Carolina's accumulating resources produced a greater variety and richness of public buildings in the mid-19th century, though the best of them were designed by architects from outside the South. By contrast, we have already seen how neighboring South Carolina was a well-established and prosperous colony with glamorous and luxurious buildings. But after about 1835, that state suffered a precipitous decline in growth and quality of architecture, though many of its best buildings were designed by native-born architects. As we explore more of the Old South in future volumes, like pieces in a puzzle, we will begin to appreciate the relationship between the history and buildings of the old, well-established coastal states, Virginia, Maryland, the Carolinas, and the rougher frontier states, Georgia, Tennessee, Alabama, Mississippi and Louisiana, as well as the region's contribution to American architecture in general.

The place to begin studying North Carolina's historic architecture is at the Survey and Planning Branch, Archaeology and Historic Preservation Section, of the North Carolina Department of Archives and History in Raleigh. Careful surveys of buildings throughout the state have been made, structures documented and evaluated, and nominations prepared for the National Register of Historic Places, under the indefatigable direction of Catherine W. Bishir. The wealth of information in the National Register files has been tremendously helpful, in particular research by Margaret Long Stephenson (Duke-Lawrence House), Walter Best (Duke-Lawrence House), Catherine W. Bishir (William Paisley Cabin, Little Manor), James Sumner (William Paisley Cabin), Davyd Foard Hood (St. Andrew's Church), Ruth Little (Holly Bend), Greer Suttlemyre (Holly Bend, Oak Lawn, Ingleside, Clover Hill), Janet K. Seapker (Orton, First Baptist Church at New Bern), Charles Blume, Jr. (Orton) and Tony P. Wren (First Baptist Church at New Bern). Interested, helpful and friendly librarians have given further encouragement and assistance, especially at the Southern Historical Collection of the University of North Carolina Library.

I. *The Colony*

In 1585 seven English ships with 106 colonists were sent by Sir Walter Raleigh to the territory which would later become North Carolina. The year before, Richard Hakluyt, scholar, diplomat and great propagandist of British colonies and one of the men to whom Raleigh later assigned his rights to what he called "Virginia," had advised would-be colonial proprietors to send "Millwrights, to make milles for spedy and cheape sawinge of timber and boardes . . . Sawyers, for common use . . . Carpenters, for buildings . . . Brick makers, Tile makers, Lyme makers, Bricklayers, Tilers, Thatchers with reedes, rushes . . . Quarrellers to digge tile, Rough Masons, Carpenters, Lathmakers."[1] Though the first colonists probably used tents, like the colonists who came to Jamestown in the summer of 1607, and had to settle for a time with huts walled with clay and reeds and roofed with bark or boughs, they soon tried to reproduce the simplest houses of England. David Glavin, an Irish soldier who landed at Roanoke Island in 1585, wrote: "There, as soon as they had disembarked, they began to make brick and tiles for a fort and houses."[2] The fort was an earthenwork construction, strengthened with palisades and surrounded by ditches. Excavations at Roanoke have uncovered bricks made of local clay, probably used for the foundations and chimneys of houses.[3] In 1591 this settlement was found mysteriously abandoned.

It was not until sixteen years later, in 1607, that the first permanent English settlement in North America was made at Jamestown in Virginia. Explorers and hunters from Virginia became the first settlers of North Carolina, which they called "South Virginia." In May and June, 1607, Gabriel Archer was busy "Pallazaoding our fort" and "cutting downe a greate oke for Clapboard." Nathaniel Batts, a young fur trader from Virginia, came to the mouth of the Chowan River in the fall of 1653. Francis Yardley wrote in May, 1654: "I dispatched away a boat with six hands, one being a carpenter, to build the [Indian] king an English house. . . . Our people built . . . a fair house, which I am to furnish with English utensils and chattels."[4] The carpenter, Robert Bodman, made two trips to North Carolina, working for five months to build Batts's two-room, timber-framed trading post, which Bodman described as "20 foote square with a lodging chamber, and a Buttery, and a chimney."[5]

In 1663 Charles II created a new colony, Carolina, when he granted all the lands between Spanish Florida and Virginia to eight political supporters. After advertising for "Carpenters, Wheel-rights, Joyners, Coopers, Bricklayers,"[6] these Lords Proprietors sent colonists to the Cape Fear River in 1664 but abandoned that outpost three years later. Meanwhile, they established a permanent settlement at the mouth of the Ashley River in the southern part of the colony in territory which would become South Carolina. The northern part of the colony, known as the Albemarle, was neglected by the Proprietors but continued to be settled by Virginians. It received a separate governor and assembly in 1712 and finally became the separate Royal province of North Carolina in 1729.

In the 1690's settlers began to come more rapidly to the North Carolina territory, and by 1694 the population was about three thousand persons. By 1710 settlements extended from the Virginia border southward to Albemarle Sound and along the Roanoke, Pamlico and Neuse rivers. John Urmston, a curmudgeonly missionary of the 1710's, called the colony "this hell of a hole . . . an obscure corner of the world inhabited by the dregs and gleanings of all other English colonies."[7] Bath, North Carolina's first town, was laid out on the banks of the Pamlico River about 1700 and incorporated in 1706. Three years later the settlement had twelve houses. Bath at first flourished and then declined in the mid-18th century. In 1710 the town of New Bern was established, where the Trent and Neuse rivers meet, by German and Swiss colonists who had come to North Carolina by way of England and Virginia, laying out the city in the form of a cross. The first colonists at New Bern included four carpenters, a mason, a locksmith, a glazier, a turner and a tilemaker. Though twenty years later New Bern was reported to have "but a few Houses or Inhabitants," it became North Carolina's principal port in the late colonial and immediate post-Revolutionary period. In 1718 a frame courthouse was built at Edenton, a settlement on Albemarle Sound near the mouth of the Chowan River, where Nathaniel Batts had built his trading post half a century earlier. The town was incorporated in 1722, and ten years later Edenton had become, with about sixty houses and a handful of warehouses, shops, offices and taverns, the province's largest town. Settlement in the lower Cape Fear Valley, which had failed in the 1690's, was resumed thirty years later. Brunswick was founded in 1725 near the mouth of the Cape Fear River, and Wilmington was founded about 1733 on the east bank farther up the river. Wilmington soon eclipsed Brunswick, which, by 1731, had dwindled to "a poor, hungry, unprovided Place, consisting of not above 10 or 12 scattered mean Houses, hardly worth the name of a Village" and was finally deserted during the Revolution.[8] By 1754 Wilmington had seventy families.

Our picture of early North Carolina building must remain indistinct, because so few buildings and documents have survived. The Carolina colonists came from a preindustrial England, a small, rural country whose domestic buildings were still constructed along medieval patterns. London was a city of wooden houses until the Great Fire of 1688. These box-like frames of rough-hewn timbers were not self-consciously designed but built according to tradition and habit. Though there were virtually no architects as we know them, skilled craftsmen specialized in house-building. About 1690 a joiner named Henry Norman in the Albemarle complained to Philip Ludwell, governor of the province between 1689 and 1694, that his Indian servant had run off with "one Carpender's broad Ax, one Joyrne squere, one payre of Joyrne Compassas, one gouge, one Joynter plane, two Ojres, one hand saw, Phile, one small Auger, two Chisell."[9]

Tar, pitch, turpentine, cypress and cedar shingles and lumber were the principal exports of colonial North Carolina. John Lawson, a surveyor and naturalist who, in the spring of 1701, settled in North Carolina, advised future colonists to bring their "Iron-work, as Nails, Spades, Axes . . . Wedges, and Saws of all sorts, with other Tools for Carpenters [and] Joiners." He reported that tulip poplars were so prodigious in size—up to ten feet in diameter—that one man even lived inside a hollow tree until his new house had been completed. Tulip poplar, Lawson wrote, made "a pretty Wainscot, Shingles for Houses, and Planks for several Uses" and chestnut trees were good for "House-Frames, Palisado's, Sills."[10] But pine, plentiful and easy to saw, was by far the favorite building material, though oak was also popular in the province. By the third quarter of the 18th century, more than fifty sawmills had been erected along the creeks of the lower Cape Fear River, where the current was strong enough to drive them and landowners had the necessary capital.[11]

The frames of wooden houses rested on a simple foundation wall made of bricks laid on the ground. Large timbers of the walls were shaped into long rectangles with a broad axe and smoothed with an adze. It might take thirty great timbers, each fifteen by twelve inches

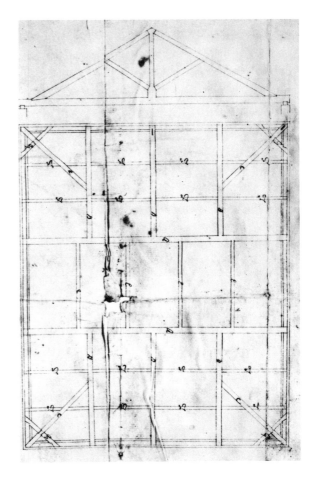

John Hawks's drawing of roof construction at the Governor's Palace, New Bern, 1767, is an example of the intricacy and beauty of timber-frame construction. *Photograph from North Carolina Division of Archives and History*

thick, to assemble a small four-room, two-story house. The heavy timbers of the frame were fitted together with mortise-and-tenon joints and held in place with wooden pegs, a technique which would be used till the second quarter of the 19th century, when lightweight, machine-milled lumber and cheap, factory-made nails became available. Each timber fitted together with a chisel, mallet and auger, the skeletal frame and roof of one of these buildings was much like the hull of a ship turned upside down, a mechanical structure which had become a work of art in the necessary care with which each part was carved and joined. The spaces between the upright studs of the walls were filled with straw, clay, brick, stone or marsh grass. The roofs were covered with thatch or shingles. Clapboards were split from logs about four to six feet long. The log was first split into quarters through its length, then further split radially into slender wedges. Chimneys were made of brick or a combination of wood and clay. Ironware, tools, nails, roof tiles, paving stone and window frames were usually imported.

It should not be surprising, however, that the oldest building in North Carolina is a brick house, for such an exceptional and durable structure would have been the most likely to survive from an era of makeshift and impermanent architecture. The so-called Newbold-White House, a one-and-one-half story brick, gable-roofed structure, faces the Perquimans River near Hertford.[12] Small but elegant, it has walls laid in Flemish bond with glazed headers, a projecting watertable, segmental window arches, low parapets and corbelled gable ends. The roof is covered with cypress shingles. The simple two-room plan of the Newbold-White House had to serve all the family's needs, for there was no separate kitchen on the property until the 19th century. This plan, with one large room adjoined by a smaller one, was really the American cousin of the all-purpose great halls and their adjacent screened passageways (like the "Buttery" mentioned by Robert Bodman in North Carolina in 1654), which continued to be the heart of the English house as it evolved in the 16th and 17th centuries.

The exact date of the Newbold-White House is unknown. The house may have been built as early as 1672 by Joseph Scott, a Quaker who came to North Carolina from England by way of Virginia, or by his son Joshua, or by William Fryley, a joiner who married Joshua's daughter, sometime shortly before 1701, or by Abraham Sanders, who bought the land in 1726. However, it is evident that a substantial house was on the land by 1689, when the county court was held at what was then the Widow Scott's house. More extensive archaeology may determine the construction date.

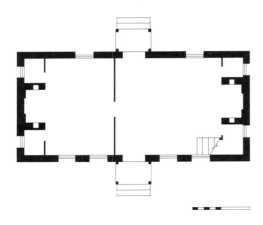

Plan of Newbold-White House.

Newbold-White House, Hertford vicinity, c. 1700.

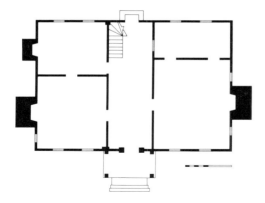

Plan of Cupola House.

Chimneypiece, Sloop Point, Pender County, second quarter of the 18th century. *Frances Benjamin Johnston, Library of Congress*

The Newbold-White House has been carefully but considerably restored. Much evidence remained of the early appearance of the exterior. Fragments of diamond-shaped quarrels and "ghost" marks in the window frames indicated the arrangement of lead casements. (Before 1700 windows were casements of diamond-shaped panes held together with lead joints. After about 1700, sash windows began to be used.) The shed dormers were rebuilt from clear evidence left in the roof structure. The stoop and front doors are completely conjectural. Inside, a 19th-century stair and hall partition were removed to recreate the original two-room plan, and the stair was rebuilt in its original location in one corner of the principal room near the chimney. The arrangement of the stair was based on marks in the plaster and floor, but its details had to be modelled on early stairs which have survived in nearby Virginia. Because the original joists had long since decayed and been replaced, there was no evidence left to indicate the width of the original flooring or whether it was nailed or pegged. The only original finish of the interior is some panelling in the attic. The Newbold-White House is open to the public.

Cupola House, at 405 South Broad Street in Edenton, is probably the oldest frame house in North Carolina, one of its most important and most puzzling houses.[13] It is now believed that Cupola House was built about 1725 for Richard Sanderson, a tobacco planter and mariner. The high gables, great projecting chimneys and broad, overhanging second story, associated with the New England colonies and otherwise unknown in the South, recall the late medieval buildings of England. In the 1750's, the original interiors of Cupola House were removed by a new owner, Francis Corbin, who wanted to "improve" it. If Cupola House was typical of its period, the great structural posts and beams of its frame probably stood out from the walls and ceilings, perhaps boxed with smooth boards. Interiors would have been plastered and whitewashed, with wainscot and doors made of flush boards or simple raised panels. The earliest surviving interior is at Sloop Point, a cottage built perhaps as early as the late 1720's for John Baptista Ashe east of Wilmington in Pender County. The treatment of the chimney breast in the original parlor, with its architrave and corner blocks, panelled overmantel flanked by pilasters and lacking a shelf, suggests what may have once been at Edenton's Cupola House. About 1731 John Brickell, a physician at Edenton, provided some further impressions of early local architecture when he wrote: "Their Houses are built after two different Ways: viz. the most substantial Planters generally use Brick and Lime, which is made of Oyster shells, for there are no Stones to be found proper for that purpose but near the Mountains; the meaner sort erect

Cupola House, 405 South Broad Street, Edenton, c. 1725.

Palmer-Marsh House, Bath, c. 1744.

with Timber, the outside with Clap-Boards. The Roofs of both Sorts of Houses are made with Shingles, and they generally have Sash Windows, and affect large and decent Rooms with good Closets. . . . Their Furniture . . . consists of Pewter, Brass, Tables, Chairs, which are imported here commonly from England."[14]

The only other large frame house to survive from the first half of the 18th century in North Carolina is the so-called Palmer-Marsh House, facing Water Street which runs along the creek in the town of Bath.[15] A two-and-one-half story frame structure with a gable roof and stone basement, the house has a four-room plan with a separate entrance from the street intended for business visitors. The house was built about 1744 for Michael Coutanch, a French-born merchant who came to North Carolina from Massachusetts in 1739, and it was owned after 1764 by Robert Palmer, Surveyor General of the province. The posts and beams of the timber frame project into the rooms. Exterior chimneys at one end are united by a brick pent, so massive that closets with windows occupy the space between them on two stories. The Palmer-Marsh House is open to the public.

North Carolina's earliest houses were inevitably imitations of those in adjacent colonies, copied from the simplest houses of England. The most common plan was the one prescribed by William Penn in 1684: "Build then, a House of thirty foot long and eighteen broad, with a partition near the middle, and an other to divide one end of the House into two small Rooms."[16] Such three-room houses, of stone, brick or wood, were box-like structures with end chimneys, a ladder or steep stair to small rooms under the gable. William Charlton's house, outside Windsor, was probably built in the late 1730's. It is the earliest surviving example of this practical and simple plan, so common in North Carolina throughout the 18th century. The handsome Flemish-bond brick walls, with arched window openings, projecting watertable and T-shaped chimneys, and the basic plan are intact, but the interior finish, the original roof and dormers were destroyed by a fire.

North Carolina's first church was a frame structure, twenty-five feet long; it was built at Edenton in 1702 by a builder named John Porter, assisted by one "Mr. Southwick."[17] William Gordon carried the plans back to England to obtain glass for the windows.[18] But it was criticized after seven years as "small, very sorrily put together and . . . ill-looked after."[19] Four years later, John Urmston, missionary in the Chowan District between 1709 and 1721, reported that this church was "ready to drop down . . . hath neither floor nor seats, only a few loose benches upon the sand, the Key being lost, the door stood open ever since I came

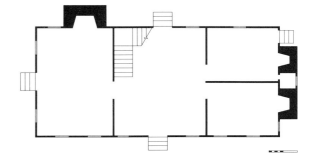

Plan of Palmer-Marsh House.

Chimneys with pent, Beaufort County.
Frances Benjamin Johnston, Library of Congress

Palmer-Marsh House, interior view.

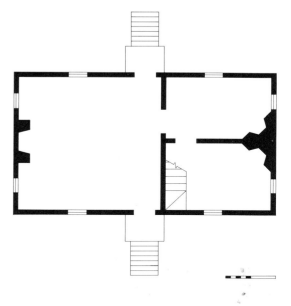

Top: William Charlton House, Windsor vicinity, c. 1735, with plan.
Bottom: St. Thomas Church, Bath, 1734–35.

St. Paul's Church, Edenton, 1736–74, steeple 1806–09.

into-the Country. All the Hoggs and Cattle flee thither for shade in the summer and warmth in Winter . . . dig holes and bury themselves . . . make it a loathsome place with their dung and nastiness."[20]

The oldest surviving church is St. Thomas, Bath, which was built for a congregation established in 1701, four years before the town was incorporated.[21] Rev. Thomas Bray of London's Society for the Propagation of the Gospel had given a fine library of one thousand religious books to the town, one of at least thirty-nine libraries he sent to America. Construction of St. Thomas Church was supervised by Rev. John Garzia, the first Anglican minister permanently resident in Bath, in 1734–35. He wrote in May, 1735, that the walls and roof of the church were "just now finished." But the church fell into decay after Garzia's death in 1744, for a new clergyman did not arrive until ten years later, and the roof and gables were destroyed during a violent storm in the mid-19th century. The one-story, two-foot thick walls of St. Thomas are laid in Flemish bond with glazed headers. The gable roof may have originally been hipped and was probably altered to provide space for galleries. Before the roof collapsed, there was a brick tower, perhaps part of the original construction. Despite considerable restoration work done in the 1940's, the church today retains many changes made over many years. The odd segmental arch over the entrance may have once framed a lunette window or part of a pediment. The interior had high box pews, a paved brick floor and a high pulpit with a sounding board.

The other surviving church from the early colonial period was the third church for St. Paul's, Edenton. The building was begun in 1736, but the roof was not in place until the summer of 1746, and the first service was not held there until April, 1760. The church was still unfinished in February, 1766, when the minister, John Barnett, wrote: "It is a very handsome brick building, upwards of seventy-one feet in length and breadth and height in proportion. The roof is finished and the Sashes, Glass, &c. will arrive from England, I hope, next winter."[22] The windows were installed about 1771, and the interior was finally finished in 1774. St. Paul's is a traditional church of the type popularized by Sir Christopher Wren and James Gibbs, a wide, boxy building with a square engaged entrance tower, low-pitched gable roof, modillion cornice and rusticated door surrounds. (Plate XXVI of Batty Langley's *City & Country Builder's & Workman's Treasury of Designs*, published in 1740, could have served as a model for these doorways.) An elliptical apse is laid in all-header bond. The steeple of St. Paul's was added by William Nichols between 1806 and 1809. The present interior, with its barrel-vaulted ceiling and side galleries supported by columns, dates from

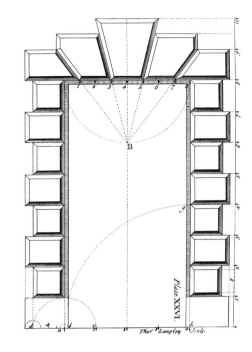

Rusticated doorway, St. Paul's Church, with its possible model, Plate XXVI of Batty Langley's *The City & Country Builder's & Workman's Treasury* (London, 1740). *Langley illustration: Houghton Library, Harvard University*

1819, with considerable restoration done after a fire in 1949. Other large brick churches were begun at New Bern in the 1740's and Brunswick in the 1750's.

When Governor Arthur Dobbs reached North Carolina in 1754, he found no satisfactory public buildings, only one church—St. Paul's—with a roof and everywhere only "little paltry houses mostly of wood."[23] There were no trained architects, for when he wanted to build a fort at Cape Lookout two years later, Dobbs protested ruefully, "As I have no Engineer here, nor know how to get one, I was obliged to act as Engineer myself & rub up my former knowledge in fortifications . . . and have accordingly drawn a plan for a square fort."[24] Perhaps more significant than their small quantity is the small scale of surviving early colonial North Carolina buildings. In addition to Cupola House at Edenton and Michael Coutanch's house at Bath, there is only one other two-story house before 1765 that we know. Milford, some seven miles east of Elizabeth City, was built in 1746. (Except for its Flemish bond walls, with stringcourses and watertable, the house has been much changed.) A young merchant from London who came to North Carolina shortly after the Revolution described the modest architecture of three coastal towns. Edenton, he wrote, had houses "most of them very indifferent and all built of wood." Washington's houses were "all wood, without either form or regularity." Wilmington, "the most disagreeable, sandy barren town," consisted of only "a few scattered wood and brick houses without any kind of order or regularity."[25]

One compromise made by the practical builders of early North Carolina was the use of brick end walls for a timber-framed house. This afforded some safety from fires which might spread from chimneys and open hearths without the trouble and expense of constructing a house entirely of brick. The so-called Sutton-Newby House, at New Hope Township in Perquimans County, was probably built for Joseph Sutton II, a planter and colonial assemblyman, about 1745. It is a one-and-one-half story structure, with end walls of brick and front and rear walls of frame construction. The brick ends are laid in Flemish bond up to the top of the first story, where the builder began laying his bricks in a triangular pattern of decorative glazed headers up to the gable end. The interior, which probably had a simple two-room plan, has been lost except for parts of the original stair, with its heavy handrail and turned balusters, and one panelled door.

Another compromise made by the builders of colonial North Carolina was the use of gambrel roofs, which provided greater headroom in attics without the expense of adding another full story. The origins of

Sutton-Newby House, New Hope Township, c. 1745. *Historic American Buildings Survey, Library of Congress*

Top: Myers-White House, Perquimans County, c. 1735. Bottom: Davenport House, with its stair, Perquimans County, c. 1750. *Historic American Buildings Survey, Library of Congress*

Top: Booth House, Edenton, c. 1760. *Frances Benjamin Johnston, Library of Congress.* Bottom: James Battle House, Nash County, c. 1790. *North Carolina Collection, University of North Carolina Library, Chapel Hill*

the gambrel roof, so early an invention that it was undocumented, are obscure. Gambrels, with their characteristic double slope, seem to have evolved as an economical way of shortening the tall gables of late medieval roofs. The American colonists called them "Dutch" roofs, indicating their belief that gambrel roofs came from the Continent or perhaps Holland, a country which contributed so much to English architecture in the early 18th century. Gambrels were certainly common in southeastern England and are found often in New Jersey, Pennsylvania, Delaware and Maryland. They appear in Virginia in the early 18th century and in North Carolina in the mid- to late 18th century. Only a handful are known in South Carolina and fewer still in Georgia. Notably, the early examples of gambrel-roofed houses in North Carolina are all only one and one-half stories high, never the two and one-half stories found in the older and richer colonies to the North.

Perquimans County has at least six gambrel-roofed houses, the last of them built in the Federal period. The Myers-White House, the earliest gambrel-roofed dwelling in the county and probably in the state, was built in the 1730's for Thomas Long, a planter. It has brick ends, with massive chimneys, and frame construction for the front and rear walls. It has a two-room plan with a stair located in a rear shed. The now-demolished Davenport House, probably built in the mid-18th century near Hertford, had a two-room plan, a handsome stair with wide handrail, turned balusters and raised panels. It also had brick ends and frame front and rear walls. Both of these houses had flush siding across the front walls under the porch. Nash County also has at least two gambrel-roofed houses. The last of them, built in the Federal period, is the James Battle House, which stands in ruins, its interior gutted.

Another grander and better-preserved gambrel-roofed house was built eight miles northwest of Windsor by William King, a cooper, carpenter and farmer who carved his initials and the date "1763" in the chimney of his new house.[26] His father, a justice of the peace in Chowan County, had settled the plantation in 1743, and some forty years later the younger King owned one thousand acres of land, eighty-four cattle, 384 hogs, fifty-one sheep, twenty-nine slaves, horses, beehives and a "parcel of fowl." King's wealth is significant, for it indicates how a North Carolina planter put his money into land, crops, livestock and slaves and not into a big house. King's house has a gambrel roof, with the typical two-room plan and brick ends. In the parlor, the chimney wall is fully panelled, with round-backed cupboards flanking the fireplace. The King House was moved about four miles to a new site in 1978 and will be opened to the public after restoration has been completed.

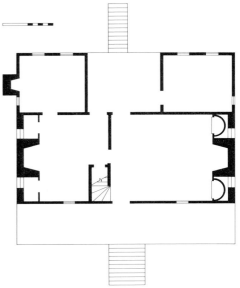

William King House, Windsor vicinity, 1763, and its plan. *Photograph, North Carolina Division of Archives and History*

William King House, parlor.

By the mid-18th century, architectural developments which had come to England a half century earlier began to reach North Carolina by way of Virginia. In the late 17th century, England had undergone rapid, if sometimes erratic, social and economic changes, bringing a small, rural, traditional country to the threshold of international prominence. Holland was then the richest and most progressive nation in Europe, with a fleet of ships twice the size of England's, and had a powerful influence on English architecture. When Royalists retreated to Holland during the English Revolution, they adopted many Continental building ideas, some elements of lively Baroque design, hipped roofs and several Dutch inventions, including stepped gables and the weight-and-pulley mechanism for sash windows. As the 18th century progressed, reflecting this Dutch influence, in England and America, roofs were more often hipped and flatter. Even in simple houses, wide, flaring eaves kicked water away from walls and windows, stringcourses strengthened the walls where floor joists were inserted, jack arches supported and shifted the weight of walls above windows, and watertables protected foundations from rainwater. This horizontality was emphasized with modillion or dentil eaves cornices. The flat, clean geometry of walls was further heightened with Flemish bond brickwork, quoins at the angles, elegant glazed headers and window arches of bright red gauged brick. Fireplaces, at first framed with a simple moulded architrave, were now more richly decorated with shelves supported by carved consoles, and panelled and pedimented overmantels. Fireplace walls, sometimes entire rooms from floor to ceiling, were panelled. In great houses, doors were framed with pilasters or engaged columns, with cornices or pediments. Stairs rose in straight flights, turned at landings, often lit by Venetian windows, and were enclosed by heavy, carved balusters and wide, flattened handrails.

Francis Corbin, born in England, visited North Carolina in the 1740's, settled there permanently as a land agent in 1750 and purchased Cupola House, Edenton, in 1756. The ambitious Corbin must have considered Cupola House, built some thirty years earlier, hopelessly old-fashioned, for he hired a carpenter named Robert Kirshaw, to whom Corbin still owed £200 when he died in 1768, to install elaborate new panelling in the self-consciously prepossessing style of mid-18th-century Georgian England. The design of these fully panelled rooms, with their commanding chimneypieces, pedimented doorways, fluted pilasters and foliated consoles, may have been inspired by William Salmon's *Palladio Londinensis*, published in 1734. Despite its elegance, the new woodwork doesn't quite fit the rooms (the ceilings have been cut out to make space for the pediments), suggesting that the carving was added as an after-

Cupola House, view of stair at second story.
Frances Benjamin Johnston, Library of Congress

Cupola House, doorways in hall, left, and parlor, right. These photographs, and those of the following two pages, illustrate the recreated rooms at Cupola House.

Cupola House, parlor.

Cupola House, dining room.

thought. In 1918 the interiors of the first story, except the walnut stair, were purchased by the Brooklyn Museum, where they were installed in the late 1920's. Forty years later, Cupola House was finally restored, with first-story rooms copied from the originals, and is now open to the public.

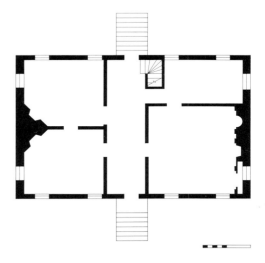

Old Brick House, Elizabeth City vicinity, c. 1760, with its plan. *Historic American Buildings Survey, Library of Congress*

Robert Kirshaw, the carpenter who worked for Francis Corbin, may also have been responsible for the robust carving at the Old Brick House, overlooking the Pasquotank River near Elizabeth City. No one has discovered any documents which might date Old Brick House, but it would appear to have been built in the late 1750's. This one-and-one-half story structure rests on a high brick and stone foundation, with end walls of brick, laid in Flemish bond with glazed headers, and front and rear walls of frame construction. Unhappily, the superb interiors were removed in the 1930's and installed, as bits and pieces, in a house in Delaware, so their original appearance is known only through photographs. Three chambers and the hall of the first story were fully panelled in a bold and simple style like the decorations at Cupola House. The hall had a dentil cornice, pulvinated frieze and raised panels above and below a moulded chairrail. In the parlor, the fireplace was embellished

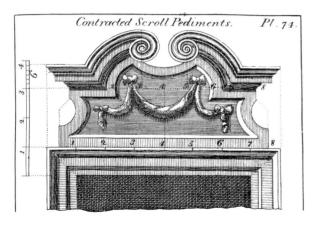

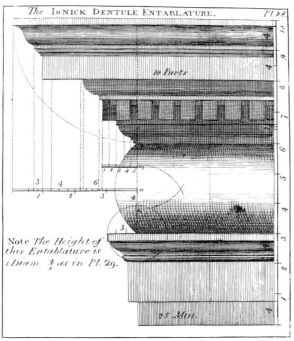

The model for details at Old Brick House, Batty Langley's *The Builder's Jewel* (London, 1741). The pediment from Plate 74 was used for a chimneypiece, and the entablature from Plate 98 was used in parlor and hall. *Houghton Library*

with a dramatic Baroque-like broken pediment, which, with the pulvinated frieze and other details, appears to have been copied from Batty Langley's *Builder's Jewel*, whose simplified designs and handy size made that builder's handbook especially popular after its publication in 1741. (The pediment over the fireplace at the Old Brick House was really intended by Langley to be used, in much smaller scale, over a door!) The fireplace was flanked by pairs of fluted Ionic pilasters and a matching cupboard and closet set into arches with ribbed keystones. Across the hall, two smaller chambers, with corner fireplaces sharing a common chimney, were also fully panelled. The cornices were simpler in these two rooms, but the builder made deep, panelled window seats in the thick, brick end walls. Only a fourth chamber, a small serving room with direct access to the attic and basement kitchen, was not fully panelled.

The so-called Shoulars House, which once stood near present-day Rich Square, was demolished more than a generation ago, when, with fragments of another house in the neighborhood, it was used to build a new "colonial" house, now a golf club, in Richmond. But the Shoulars House must have been a small jewel. Its gambrel roof had a modillion eaves cornice, and the brick ends, laid in Flemish bond, had a moulded brick watertable, brilliant glazed headers and segmental window openings. The chimney wall in the parlor was fully panelled, with a cupboard made so much like fine furniture that it could slide from its niche in the fireplace wall.

In 1747 John Duke, a Virginian, had built a one-and-one-half story frame house near the present-day hamlet of Roxobel, an area of Quaker settlement. Some twenty years later—the date is uncertain—his son-in-law John Lawrence made a two-story brick addition. Again, beautifully finished interiors have been removed and their original appearance is known only through old photographs. But what a wonder they were! The hall had a closed-string stair, with elaborately turned balusters, and panelled wainscot. In other rooms, entire fireplace walls were embellished with up to six tiers of raised panels, some designed to accommodate the segmental arches of the fireplaces, so typical of the late 18th-century Southern frontier. Other walls in these rooms had plaster over panelled wainscot. The panelling was painted to simulate mahogany or walnut.

North Carolina was now ready to afford even more stylish buildings. Between 1730 and 1770 the population of the province increased nearly six-fold. Tobacco in the northeastern counties and rice along the creeks of the lower Cape Fear River were becoming rich crops. New Bern on the Neuse River was becoming the principal port. Soon a public wharf

Old Brick House, parlor. *Private Collection*

Old Brick House, first-story chamber. *Private Collection*

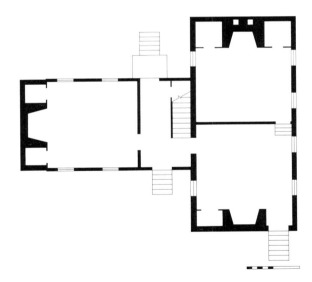

Top: Shoulars House, Rich Square vicinity, c. 1760. *Private Collection*. Bottom: John Duke/John Lawrence House, Roxobel vicinity, 1747, enlarged c. 1765, with its plan.

Shoulars House, parlor. *Private Collection*

Duke-Lawrence House, stairhall. *Private Collection*

Duke-Lawrence House, interior panelling. *Private Collection*

Duke-Lawrence House, interior panelling. *Private Collection*

was built, with merchants' offices crowding along Craven Street and the waterfront. North Carolina's first newspaper, the *North Carolina Gazette*, was established there in 1751. And an ambitious new Royal Governor, William Tryon, who reached New Bern in October, 1764, brought the grander ideas of English Palladianism to the colony.

When George I ascended the throne in 1714, a wealthy Whig aristocracy had come to power. These new tastemakers rejected the elaborate Baroque architecture associated with the Stuart kings in favor of a more severe style based on the writings of the late 16th-century Italian designer Andrea Palladio, known primarily through one famous work, *The Four Books of Architecture*, an illustrated guide on how to build like the ancient Romans. The first English edition of Palladio was published by Giacomo Leoni in installments between 1716 and 1720. In 1719 Lord Burlington, the greatest sponsor of Palladianism in England, returned with his protégé William Kent from a trip to the Veneto of Italy where they had seen Palladio's buildings. Palladio had used Roman temples as the model for many of his buildings, and the most prominent hallmarks of so-called Palladian buildings were the use of columns, pediments or projecting pavilions to suggest a giant temple portico, as well as raised first floors, balanced wings, or flankers, and Venetian windows. (A Venetian, or Palladian, window is a large, round-headed window flanked by smaller rectangular windows.)

When Tryon became Governor in March, 1765, he must have been eager to begin public works. The province had no permanent capital, the public records were scattered, the Assembly was meeting at various towns and the Governor had no official residence. Tryon had brought with him from England an architect, John Hawks. Born in Lincolnshire in 1731, Hawks had trained with Stiff Leadbetter, a Buckinghamshire carpenter and builder who succeeded Henry Flitcroft as Surveyor of St. Paul's Cathedral in London in 1756. Little is known of Hawks's life in America, except that he was made Collector of the Port at Beaufort in July, 1767, married the daughter of the provincial Secretary in 1769 and was later Clerk of the Governor's Council. He seems to have enjoyed a reputation for honesty and reliability which outlived his close association with the controversial Royal Governor, for he continued in government service after the Revolution. When Hawks died in 1791, he owned eleven unidentified "Books on Architecture."[27]

In January, 1767, the colonial Assembly voted funds for construction of government buildings at New Bern, which Tryon had selected as the colonial capital. The buildings would contain the Governor's residence, legislative hall and public offices. Hawks was hired to prepare "all necessary designs, plans, Elevations, proportions, drawings," to order and receive all materials, and to hire, supervise and pay the workmen.[28] Contracts for brick, lime and lumber were made in New Bern, but Tryon, complaining that North Carolina had no artisans skilled enough to build his mansion and capitol, dispatched Hawks to Philadelphia with a letter of introduction to find craftsmen and materials for the work.[29] Bricks were made at a kiln on the banks of nearby Lawson's Creek, but sashes, locks, hinges and chimneypieces came from England. The first bricks were laid in August, 1767. By January, 1769, the window frames and sashes were in place and the roof and gutters had been finished with eight tons of lead by "an able hand sent purposely over from London," and joiners were at work on the interior. Tryon moved into the building in June, 1770, though it was still incomplete.[30] When the Assembly met there for the first time in December, the event was celebrated with fireworks, a bonfire, and a "great Plenty of Liquor" for the populace. Tryon congratulated himself and North Carolina on having created what he called "a public ornament and credit to the colony as well as an honor to British America."[31]

Extraordinary in scale and richness as the Governor's Palace was for North Carolina, it would have been a fairly ordinary building in England, a handsome but academic copy of a Palladian country house, with its pedimented pavilion, hipped roof, quadrant passageways and matching dependencies. Houses of this type had been illustrated in Plate 63 of James Gibbs's *A Book of Architecture*, 1728, in Plates 54 and 55 of Isaac Ware's *A Complete Body of Architecture*, 1756, and Plate 11 of Robert Morris's *Select Architecture*, 1757. Hawks's teacher, Stiff Leadbetter, had already used this conventional design as the model for Nuneham Park, a country house built on the banks of the Thames near Oxford between 1756 and 1764, while Hawks was still his assistant. (Nuneham Park was later illustrated in the fifth volume of *Vitruvius Britannicus*, published by John Woolfe and James Gandon in 1771, but, since Tryon's Palace had already been completed by that year, Hawks must have relied on other books or memories of his English experience.) Hawks's preliminary drawings for the Palace, formerly at the New-York Historical Society, are now at the Historical Society of the Episcopal Church, Austin, Texas, and the final plans, submitted for approval to the Board of Trade in London, are at the British Public Record Office. In successive versions, Hawks enlarged the building from one to two rooms in depth, reduced the height from three to two stories and replaced his initial idea for a prominent Venetian window and frontispiece with a projecting central pavilion, another Palladian motif.

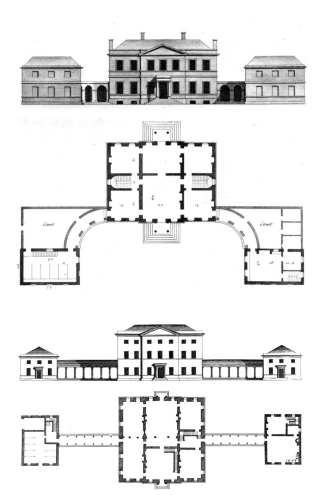

Palladian house designs from James Gibbs's *Book of Architecture* (London, 1728) and Robert Morris's *Select Architecture* (London, 1757). *Gibbs illustration: Houghton Library. Morris illustration: Avery Architectural and Fine Arts Library, Columbia University.*

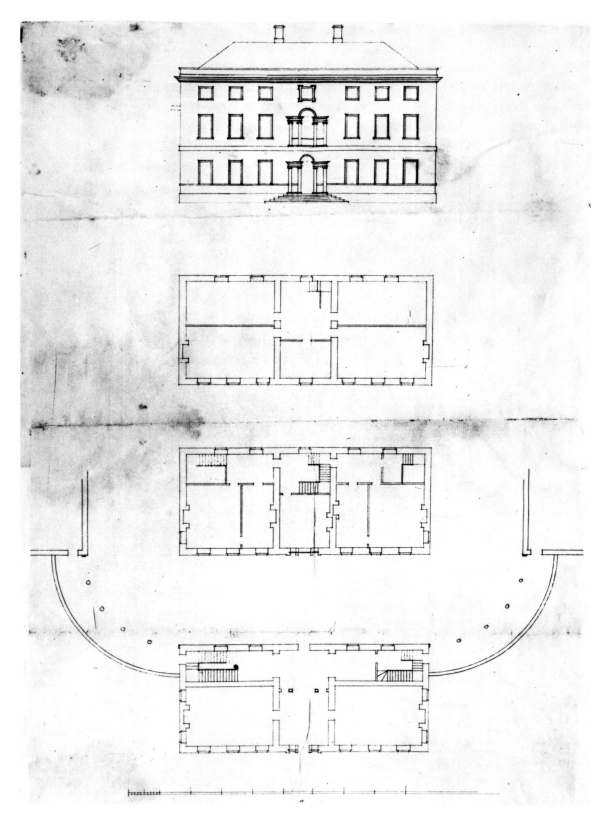

Preliminary design for Governor's Palace, c. 1767, by John Hawks.
Photograph, North Carolina Archives and History

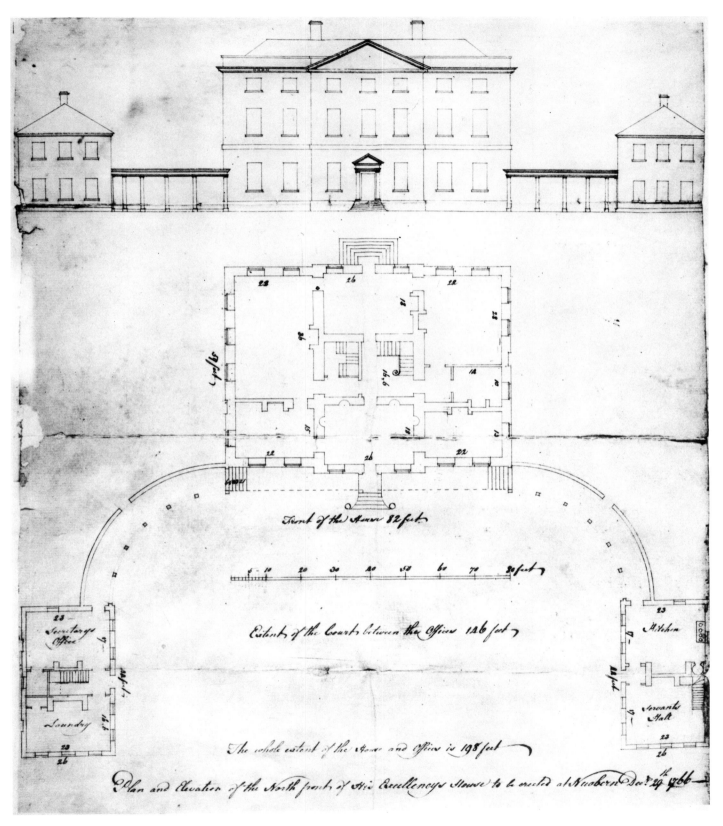

Preliminary design for Governor's Palace, c. 1767, by John Hawks. *Photograph, North Carolina Archives and History*

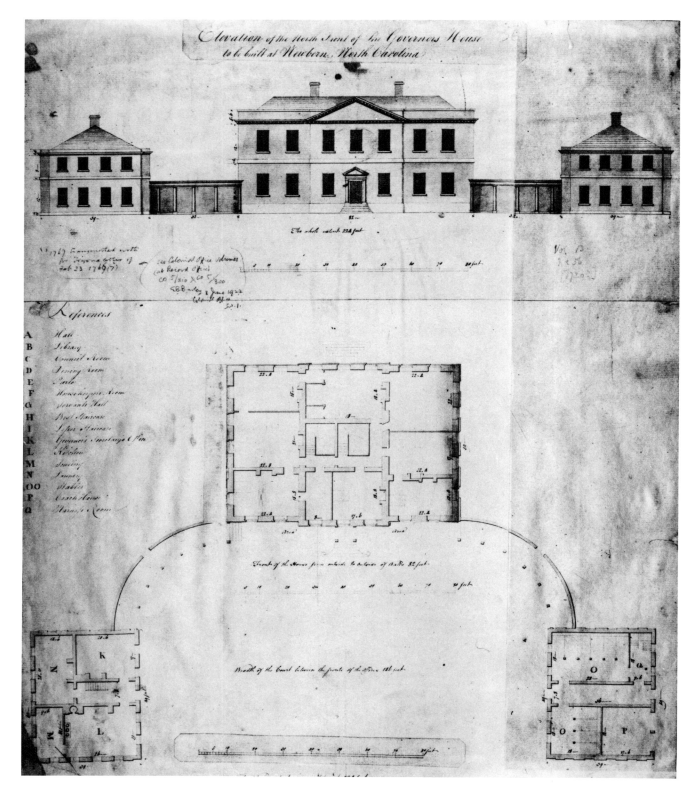

Final design for Governor's Palace, c. 1767, by John Hawks.
Photograph, North Carolina Archives and History

The Palace, two and one-half stories high, was a hip-roofed structure, with walls laid in Flemish bond and a pedimented, projecting central pavilion. (The earliest representation of the Palace as built, two stories high, appears on the face of a counterfeit £5 bill which was issued in 1775.) The Royal arms of George III were placed in the pediment.[32] The first story contained library, council room, parlor and drawing rooms, two staircases and servants' rooms. The second story contained seven residential chambers for the Governor. Quadrant passageways with colonnades led to two flankers containing the office of the Governor's secretary, kitchen, laundry, stables and coach house. Builder's estimates included mahogany for a stair, skylights and "Six Stacks of Lead Pipes." An entrance court was formed by a "Dwarf wall, Pallisadoes, Gates, &c."[33] In 1778, Ebenezer Hazzard visited the Palace: "You enter a Hall in which are four Niches for Statues. . . . Immediately on getting into the Entry you see an Elegant Stair Case with Mahogany Banisters, which reaches to the top of the House & is there covered by a glazed Cupola. . . . The Rooms are spacious, elegant & neatly finished."[34] One of Hawks's surviving drawings shows the details of one chamber. The four principal chimneypieces were ordered from England. The one in the Council Chamber, made by John Devall of London, who had worked at several buildings designed by Henry Flitcroft, was described as "A large statuary Ionic chimneypiece, the shafts of the columns sienna and the frett on the Frieze inlaid with the same; A rich edge and Foliage on the Tablet; medals of the King & Queen on the Frieze over the Columns, the moulding enriched, a large statuary marble slab and black marble covings."[35] The main block had a lead roof, but the wings, perhaps as an economy, were covered with wooden shingles, which Tryon called "a covering, when well executed & painted, more beautiful than Slate or Tyle."[36]

Governor Tryon left North Carolina in 1771, when he was appointed Governor of New York. The Palace, so extravagant a building for so poor a colony, had already become a symbol of discontent among the underrepresented small farmers and frontiersmen, who objected to paying taxes for a building they would never see or use. During the Revolution metal was removed from the Palace roof and replaced with leaky wooden shingles. In November, 1779, the Palace sustained daily damage "by reason of the lead in several places of the roof being cracked and otherways so much out of repair that every shower of rain runs through."[37] The Assembly stopped meeting regularly at New Bern after 1779, and Hillsborough served as a working government center until Raleigh became capital in 1794. When President Washington dined at

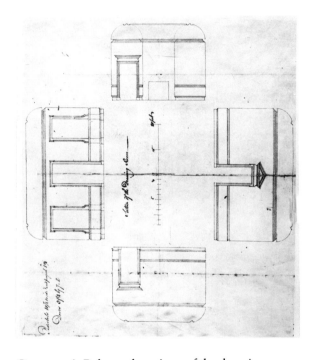

Governor's Palace, elevations of the drawing room, by John Hawks. *Photograph, North Carolina Archives and History*

Design of cupola intended for St. Paul's Church, Edenton, by John Hawks, 1769. *Hawks Papers, Southern Historical Collection, University of North Carolina, Chapel Hill.*

the Palace in 1791 he described it, in his usual laconic style, as "a good brick building but now hastening to Ruins."[38] In 1794 the legislature offered the Palace for sale, and in the meantime it was being used as a rooming house, dance hall and school.[39] In February, 1798, hay stored in the basement caught fire. The wings were saved only by demolishing the passageways leading from the burning center of the Palace. One wing was later destroyed, but the other survived, an important reference used in the 1950's for recreation of the Palace, which is now open to the public. In quality and scale of design, materials and craftsmanship, the original Palace was surely the grandest public building in any colony south of Virginia.

But what of other works by John Hawks in North Carolina? It would seem likely that he was the architect of many of the public works under construction in the late 1760's—the academy at New Bern, the courthouse and jail at Beaufort, the courthouse at Edenton, a church at Wilmington, the jail and jailor's house at New Bern, public warehouses for flax and hemp at Halifax and Campbleton, a courthouse at Salisbury. In 1766 Hawks designed improvements to Edenton's public market, a two-story brick structure, like many typical 18th-century English town halls, with an open arcade at the ground floor. In June, 1767, commissioners for building a new courthouse at Edenton had "a plan . . . 68 feet by 45" in hand when they advertised for a builder.[40] We have a drawing by Hawks for the cupola of a church at Edenton, possibly St. Paul's, dated November, 1769. The cupola was not built on the church, but a virtually identical one was built on the courthouse, which was not completed until the mid-1770's. Hawks's plan and elevation for a jail at Edenton, dated June, 1773, have also survived. It would seem unlikely that Hawks would have been asked to design only one—and the less important one—of the county's government buildings. In September, 1773, Hawks, the architect at work, sent a letter to Joseph Hewes, a merchant from New Jersey who had come to North Carolina about 1760 and who was, in 1766, appointed one of the five trustees for building the courthouse and jail at Edenton: "To the plan of the Colonnade I have drawn a double row of Columns, and pillasters and Groin Arches, which would make the Job more complete; but to this there are two objections. One is it would amount to three times the sum, the other if I rightly recollect the inside range of columns would be almost or quite close to the first Step of the court, which may be thought an obstruction to the passing and repassing."[41] This is believed to be a reference to a proposed arrangement of the courtroom, with its chair for the presiding

Courthouse, Edenton, 1767–c. 1775.

Courthouse, Edenton, second-story hall. *Frances Benjamin Johnston, Library of Congress*

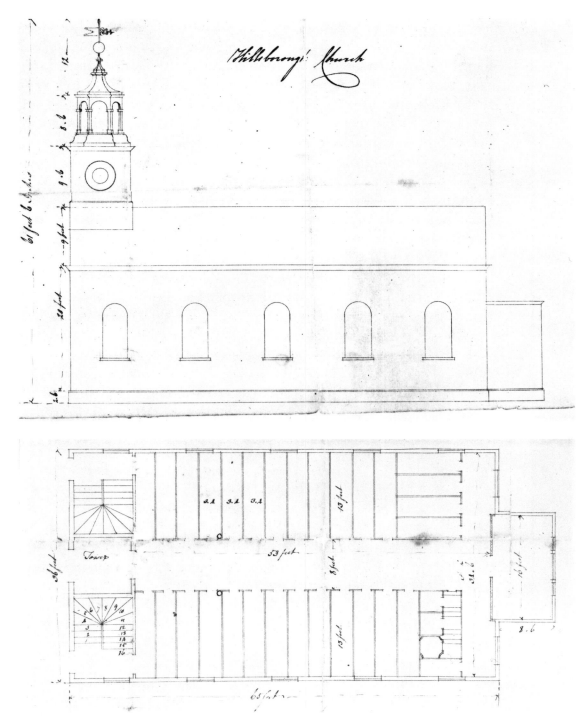

Elevation and plan of church at Hillsborough, attributed to John Hawks, c. 1768.
Southern Historical Collection, University of North Carolina

magistrate set in a semicircular apse. An upstairs meeting hall has fully panelled walls and a moulded chairrail.

Two other drawings, believed to be by Hawks, showing a plan and elevation for St. Matthew's Church, Hillsborough, have also survived. In February, 1768, the church's building committee advertised in Williamsburg for a builder.[42] St. John's Church, Williamsboro, a large, two-story barn-like frame structure with a gable roof and a low brick foundation, may also have been the work of Hawks. The church's rector, James McCartney, had been a teacher at the New Bern Academy before his ordination, and the building contract, dated October, 1771, has turned up among Hawks family papers. The builder was John Lynch of Virginia. The contract describes the interior: "The inside of the Church shall be wainscoted all around the Height of the Pews with Good pine plank . . . & to each Pew a good Pannell Door to be Hung. . . . In the East end of the Church shall be a good Communion Table . . . neatly Bannister'd & Pailed in with a good Bannister Door in the front. . . . Within the said Church shall be a Good Reading Desk with a Genteel Pulpit . . . with a neat sound at a proper Height over the Pulpit. . . . Round the said Church . . . shall be a neat Cornish. The whole inside of the Church except the wainscot, Cornish, &c. shall be well plastered with lime mortar with Sufficient Quantity of Cow's Hair mixed therein & well white washed. The Pews, Desks, Pulpit, Bannisters, Cornish & every part of the wooden work exposed to view shall be well painted of a Cream Collour."[43] The church was completed in August, 1773. When the interior was restored in 1956, a barrel-vaulted ceiling was uncovered. Except for the doors of the box pews, all church fittings have been reproduced.

Bellair, a Palladian house outside of New Bern, was built in the early 1770's and has been attributed to Hawks because of its academic style. At first glance, this three-story brick house, with its high basement, hipped roof, central pavilion, with bull's-eye window in its pediment, a moulded brick watertable and Flemish bond walls, appears to be a country house of grand scale. But the building is only one room deep, and the interior seems to have been left incomplete. The stair, with the simplest of Georgian details, is clumsily arranged, suggesting that plans for a prouder hall may have been discarded. Perhaps pre-Revolutionary disturbances forced the builder to change his plans, or perhaps the place was always intended as a country villa for brief visits. Like some other houses in the neighborhood, Bellair has cochineal foundations. The original pedimented, one-bay entrance porch was replaced in the mid-19th century.

John Burgwin, born in England in 1731, came to North Carolina by

Bellair, New Bern vicinity, c. 1770, chimneypiece.
Frances Benjamin Johnston, Library of Congress

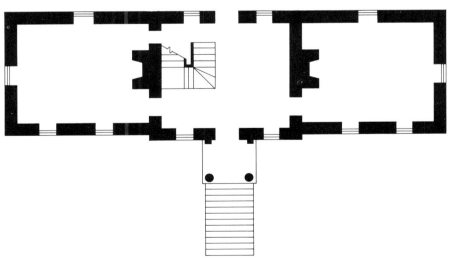

Bellair, with its plan. The porch is a 19th-century replacement.
North Carolina Archives and History

John Burgwin House, Wilmington, c. 1771. Fluted Ionic columns replace original pillars. *Frances Benjamin Johnston, Library of Congress*

way of Charleston about 1750. By the 1760's he had become a successful merchant in Wilmington, the owner of at least five ships, and a colonial official, serving as private secretary to the Governor, Clerk of the Superior Court in New Hanover County and Treasurer of the province. About 1771, Burgwin built a house at the corner of Third and Market streets in Wilmington, using as a foundation the stone walls which had been the first floor and cellar of an old jail. (The door and window openings of this foundation, one of them still retaining heavy iron bars, are unrelated to the plan of Burgwin's house.) The principal original embellishment of the exterior is a handsome Palladian frontispiece. The two-tiered porch was originally supported by simple square pillars, which were replaced with Roman Ionic columns about 1850 by a later owner, Thomas Wright, who also added rooms at the rear of the house for his eleven children. A newly discovered photograph, made about 1846, shows the early appearance of the house before these changes were made. The interior of the first story has been extensively reconstructed, but the walnut stair, with its turned balusters, and two fine upstairs chambers, one with half-domed niches and fluted pilasters, and the other with a panelled fireplace wall, are original. The house is open to the public.[44]

The famous John Wright Stanly House in New Bern was probably begun during the spring and summer of 1779 for Thomas Ogden and completed in the early 1780's for John Wright Stanly. Stanly was born in Virginia in 1742. After starting his merchant career in Jamaica and Philadelphia, he married a lady from New Bern and settled there as a merchant, maintaining his own wharf and cultivating two hundred acres in corn, indigo, rice, potatoes and cotton. The two-story frame house has a wood-shingled roof with balustrade and deck. The exterior is finished with flush siding and quoins to suggest masonry. The first-story windows are surmounted with pulvinated friezes and pediments, and the entrance has a commanding frontispiece with fanlight, Doric columns and pediment. Inside, the hall widens behind an arch to contain a mahogany stair, with turned balusters and carved step-ends. Stanly's principal trading connections were with Philadelphia, where he and his family moved during 1781–82. Perhaps the interiors of the house were completed by craftsmen from that influential city? Originally located at the corner of Middle and New streets, the Stanly house has been twice moved, once in 1933 when it was converted into a public library, and again in 1966, when its restoration was begun. The front rooms are mostly original, but the rear rooms have been reconstructed, more according to preconceptions than documentation.[45] The house, now at 307 George Street, is open to the public.

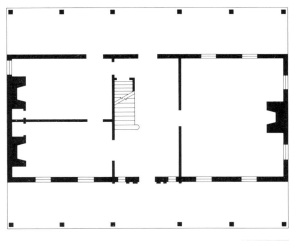

Top: The original appearance of John Burgwin House, in a detail from a 19th-century photograph. *Amon Carter Museum, Fort Worth.* Bottom: Plan of Burgwin House.

John Burgwin House, stair. *Frances Benjamin Johnston, Library of Congress*

John Burgwin House, second-story parlor. *Frances Benjamin Johnston, Library of Congress*

John Burgwin House, second-story chamber. *Frances Benjamin Johnston, Library of Congress*

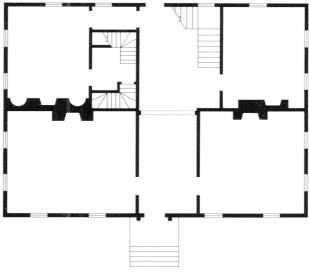

John Wright Stanly House, 307 George Street, New Bern, begun 1779, with its plan.

John Wright Stanly House, hall and, opposite page, detail of stair.

II. *Across the Frontier*

North Carolina log house, illustrated in Frederick Law Olmsted's *Journey in the Seaboard Slave States* (New York, 1856). *North Carolina Collection, University of North Carolina*

At the end of the 17th century, small farmers and indentured servants from Virginia began to move into the northern part of Carolina, and Scotch Highlanders had come as early as 1729 to the upper Cape Fear River where they established a settlement which would become the town of Fayetteville. Soon a flood of settlers began to move from Pennsylvania down the Shenandoah Valley, along the Blue Ridge into the piedmont of the interior of the Carolinas and Georgia.[1] Most of Rowan County's German pioneers came from Lancaster and Bucks counties of Pennsylvania, settling on the Yadkin River and Second Creek. As early as the 1740's, the Scotch-Irish, Protestants who had come from Scotland by way of Ireland, settled along the Hico, Eno and Haw rivers. In the 1750's and 1760's, the Moravians, survivors of religious persecution in present-day East Germany and Czechoslovakia, established five towns, the most important of which was Salem.

After the end of the French and Indian War in 1763, settlement of interior North Carolina was resumed. Three years later, Lieutenant Governor William Tryon wrote: "Last autumn and winter, upwards of one thousand wagons passed thro' Salisbury with families from the northward to settle in this province chiefly."[2] In 1729 there had been 30,000 whites in North Carolina, and by 1752 there were 50,000. In 1765 there were 120,000 in the province and on the eve of the Revolution there were 265,000. In July, 1765, Robert Jones wrote of North Carolina frontiersmen: "The Inhabitants were hospitable in their way, live in Plenty & Dirt, are stout, of great Prowess at manual Athletics, & in private conversation bold, impertinent & vain."[3] It was a world of Saturday night frolics, shooting matches and horse-racing. Reverend Charles Woodmason wrote in 1766: "The manners of North Carolinians in general are vile & corrupt. The whole country is a stage of debauchery, dissoluteness & corruption. . . . The people are composed of the Outcasts of all the other Colonies. . . . Polygamy is very common. . . . Bastardy is no disrepute, concubinage general!"[4] Waightstill Avery saw a drunken brawl at a tavern between Halifax and Hillsborough in 1769: "All blunder'd, bawl'd, spew'd and curs'd, broke one another's Heads and their own shins, with stools, and bruised their Hips and Ribs . . . pulled hair, lugg'd, hallo'd, swore, fought and kept up the Roar-Rororum till morning!"[5]

The log cabin was the ubiquitous dwelling of the early American frontier. Colonial timber-frame construction used square timbers, fitted together in a complicated pattern with wooden pegs. The log cabin was made by laying logs horizontally, fitting them together at the corners with simple notched joints, so that each log was held in place by the weight of the log above it. The log cabin may have wasted wood, which was plentiful in the frontier, but it saved labor, which was scarce. The true log cabin had been unknown to the earliest colonists or the American Indians and was brought to the Delaware Valley by Swedish settlers in the mid-17th century.

Notched joints of log construction at William Paisley Cabin, Mebane vicinity, c. 1801.

In early North Carolina, even in coastal areas where timber-frame construction was most common, log structures were often used for outbuildings and jails. In 1676, during Culpepper's Rebellion, Thomas Miller was imprisoned in a "Logg-house about 10 or 11 foot square." Seth Sothel, Governor of the Albemarle region in the 1680's, had a log house built by a carpenter named Nicholas Gent.[6] William Byrd, the witty, haughty and land-hungry Virginia squire who came to North Carolina in 1728, wrote: "Most of the houses in this part of the country are log houses, covered with pine or cypress shingles, three feet long and one broad. They hang upon lathes with pegs, and their doors, too, turn upon wooden hinges and have wooden locks to secure them, so that the building is finished without nails or other ironwork. . . . A citizen is here counted extravagant if he has ambition enough to aspire to a brick chimney!"[7] This high-handed hyperbole was verified by William Logan, who wrote in 1745: "The Common people's houses here are in general tarred all over to preserve them instead of Painting & all have Wooden Chimneys."[8]

In 1754, when twenty neighbors gathered to help Hans Wagner, a settler on the banks of the Elkin River, raise the frame of a new log house, a neighbor observed ruefully, "Things never go well at such a gathering, for more time is spent in drinking brandy than in working!"[9] In 1755, Governor Arthur Dobbs explored the interior of North Carolina. At Salisbury he found large, barefooted families of Scotch-Irish settlers from Pennsylvania living in seven or eight log houses.[10] "Their method upon entering their Lands," he wrote, "is to cut down, where they build their Log houses, all the Trees fit for Logs near their

McIntyre Cabin, Charlotte vicinity, undocumented. *Frances Benjamin Johnston, Library of Congress*

Houses."[11] After ordering construction of log houses for his soldiers,[12] twenty-seven miles west of Salisbury, Dobbs built a log fort, garrisoned with forty-six men, as a central refuge for the back-country settlers.[13] Francis Brown, who went to inspect frontier defenses in 1756, described the fort: an "Oblong Square fifty-three feet by forty, the opposite Angles [corner bastions] Twenty-four feet and Twenty-two, In height Twenty-four and a half feet. . . . The Thickness of the Walls, which are made of Oak Logs, regularly Diminished from sixteen Inches to Six. . . . It contains three floors."[14]

Though there are many cabins throughout North Carolina, few of them date from the 18th century. The so-called McIntyre Cabin, which stood eight miles north of Charlotte until its destruction in 1941, is undocumented. Logs, cut into square timbers, were laid with dovetailed notches on a fieldstone foundation. Because logs could not be arranged conveniently to form gable ends, a sawed frame and weatherboarding were used to build the upper parts of the end walls. Like so many other cabins, this one had a simple one-room plan, with dirt floor, no windows and a ladder leading to a sleeping loft. Gaps between the logs were filled with clay, but rotting logs and eroding clay were always a problem. Settlers experimented with building wider eaves or covering the walls with plaster or weatherboards.

Robert Cleveland's cabin, near Purlear, has a two-room plan, fieldstone foundation and chimneys and a ladder to the loft. Room sizes were limited by the length of straight tree trunks which did not taper too much, about twenty-five feet. So here the builder pieced the ends of his logs together to make a two-room house. The window openings were added later, but even then they were left unglazed, closed only with shutters. The walls were raised several feet above the ceiling joists before the gable roof was begun, allowing for greater headroom in the attic.

The White-Siddle Cabin in Caswell County has two log rooms connected by a wide, open passageway, now enclosed, which served as sitting room and dining room in warm weather. This open hall also served as a kennel for the family dog, giving to this house form the delightful soubriquet of dogtrot cabin. William Paisley's cabin, in the vicinity of Mebane, was built about 1801 for a Presbyterian minister, teacher and farmer. The original three-room cabin shares a chimney with another log room, added at a later time. The two structures, held up by the old chimney between them, are much like two saddlebags suspended over a horse's back, and so structures of this type are often called saddlebag cabins. The interior, unexpectedly, is finished with carefully sawed flush boards and a moulded chairrail.

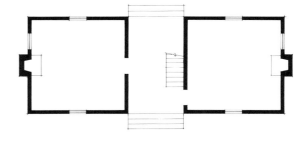

White-Siddle Cabin, two rooms with a central breezeway, Caswell County, undocumented, with its plan. *Photograph from North Carolina Archives and History, plan by Martin Meek.*

William Paisley Cabin, Mebane vicinity, c. 1801.

The Moravians were the indomitable survivors of two hundred years of religious persecution who made their way from present-day Czecho-slovakia and East Germany to North Carolina in the mid-18th century. Their missionaries had already gone to remote Greenland, Surinam, the Gold Coast, Algeria, Russia and Ceylon. After attempting to establish an outpost in the infant colony of Georgia in 1736, a group of Moravians moved to Pennsylvania in 1740. (At most there had been thirty Moravians in Georgia; by 1742 there were 120 of them at Bethlehem in Pennsylvania.) Eager to find a home of their own in America, the Moravians purchased a tract of 100,000 acres, which they called Wachovia, from the heirs of the last of the original Proprietors of Carolina. Among the first fifteen Moravians who came to North Carolina in the fall of 1753, there were two carpenters, one from Norway and another from Holstein.[15]

By 1760 there were eight married couples and thirty-eight single men living at Bethabara, the first Moravian village in North Carolina, occupying some ten buildings, including a congregation house, brothers house, tailor's shop, pottery and brick kilns, wash house, drying house, kitchen, joiner's shop, stable, distillery and bakery. About half of these buildings were timber-framed structures and half were log cabins. A three-story, half-timber mill, for processing corn, cotton and wood, was built in 1755–56, with brick nogging inserted between the spaces of its wooden frame and a tile roof. In July, 1756, the threat of Indian trouble had become so ominous that all work except harvesting was suspended so that a palisade wall could be built around the village. In 1759, another town, Bethania, was established nearby, but further settlement of Wachovia was delayed until the end of the French and Indian War four years later. In 1763, there were seventy-three settlers at Bethania and seventy-seven at Bethabara.[16]

Though they were not the most numerous of the German settlers of North Carolina, the Moravians made by far the most distinctive contribution to life—and architecture—along the frontier. Unlike many of the newcomers, they were accomplished craftsmen. In May, 1754, John Jacob Fries, minister at Bethabara, exclaimed: "I made the top of a Table for myself and . . . cut Wood for feet on the Table. They shall be Lyons Claws. . . . One day I am a Joiner, the next a Carver! What could I not learn if I was not too old!"[17] Unlike the self-sufficient, fiercely independent Scotch-Irish Presbyterians and Baptist settlers, the Moravians were dependent on a highly organized, disciplined community life. As one of their early leaders wrote in defense of their self-sacrifices: "We are indeed a group of pilgrims, and this thought lies at the foundation of our

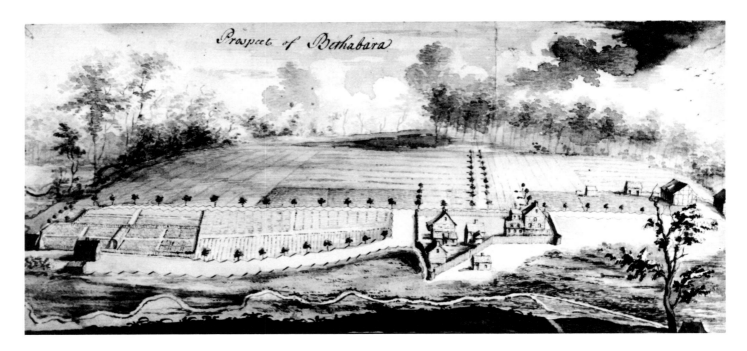

The Moravian settlement at Bethabara and the nearby half-timber mill.
Archiv der Unität Brüdergemein, Herrnhut

establishment."[18] The settlement in North Carolina was planned by Moravian church authorities in Germany, Holland, England and Pennsylvania, who decided where towns would be established, how they would be built and who would govern them. A local Board of Overseers supervised many aspects of daily life among the Moravians, especially at the town of Salem, where only Church members could reside. The Church itself owned the community store, tannery, mill, tavern and pottery. Single men and single women were employed in collective shops and lived in separate dormitories. No individual could start a business, enter a trade or open a shop without permission. The authorities planned, approved and supervised the construction of every public building, often devised with plans far more ingenious than those of the English settlers. The Moravians would gather to celebrate construction of these buildings, with sermons, prayers, hymn-singing and trumpet-playing. Each householder leased his land from the Church, whose authorities also approved the location, design and materials for private buildings. The Church's Board of Overseers supervised the craftsmen, their apprentices, the rates of pay and the standards of their work. In September, 1786, for example, the authorities decided that roof tiles should henceforth be made "a little thicker, a little wider and an inch shorter."[19]

In 1763 the authorities in Europe appointed Frederick William Marshall to be the Administrator of the Moravian settlements in Wachovia. Born in Dresden in 1721, Marshall had grown up expecting to become a court official or, like his father, a soldier. But he joined the Moravian Church at the age of nineteen and, after studying at the university at Leipzig, went to England, where he remained off and on for fifteen years with the Moravians.[20] Marshall moved to Pennsylvania in 1761, made his first trip to North Carolina in 1764–65 and finally settled there with his wife in 1768. Official records tell us about many sketches and designs shown or made by Marshall over almost forty years, and so he has been given credit for the design of most of the Moravian public buildings in North Carolina, but it is also possible that he may have merely submitted, as Administrator, the designs actually prepared by others. Marshall lived in North Carolina until his death in 1802, a few days after his eighty-first birthday.

After his appointment in 1763, Marshall's first great task was to lay out and build the central trading town for Wachovia.[21] Though they were isolated in a frontier of forests, trading paths and a few slovenly villages clustering 'round cow tracks, it was typical of the Moravians that they would devise an orderly plan for this new town, which they named Salem. The plan was based on drawings which Brother Marshall

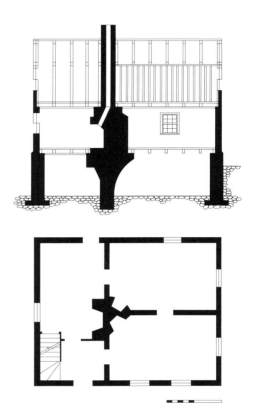

The plan and sectional view of the Distiller's House at Bethabara, 1803, an example of the ingenious and practical design of Moravian buildings.

or another unidentified artist made in July, 1765, of two Moravian cities, Niesky and Gnadenberg, in Silesia. These drawings showed a central square surrounded by lots reserved for the future public buildings of the town—the Congregation House, Church, Boys and Girls schools, Widows House, Single Sisters House on one side and Widowers House, Single Brothers House and Store on the other side. Public planning was always a vital aspect of life at Salem. A building code of 1788 codified a philosophy which had guided Salem's growth for twenty years: "In consideration of the whole picture of the Community, we have to see that the worst houses are not standing on the best lots. The same consideration has to be taken with all hazardous, noisy, disease-producing or foul-smelling trades. Wood sheds or little huts do not belong on the main street, unless they get a nice exterior."[22] Salem also had a fire inspector and a public waterworks in the 18th century.

The streets and square of Salem were laid out in February, 1766, by Christian Gottlieb Reuter, the official surveyor. Born in Germany in 1717, the son of a surgeon, Reuter had come to North Carolina by way of London and Pennsylvania in July, 1758. In April, 1766, he was made building inspector of Salem, responsible for laying out the town, constructing houses, supervising and paying workmen. An accomplished draftsman, he designed Salem's buildings before Brother Marshall finally arrived. In later years, Reuter wanted to start a drawing school and his house contained a room in the front for his sketching.[23] He was also a roadmaster, builder of the waterworks and a forest ranger. He died in 1777.

When the Moravians prepared to build Salem in 1766, they faced a dilemma. The timber near the new town was too short for log construction, but the supply of lime was too limited for making mortar for brick walls.[24] They would have to use short timbers to build frames helping to support bricks or other material which would have to be laid up with clay instead of lime mortar. Johann Ettwein reported in early 1766: "Since the trees in the vicinity of Salem are not so suitable for log houses as for half-timbered construction, we determined to build the houses chiefly of half-timbered construction."[25] Brother Reuter drew the plan for Salem's first timber-framed house in March, 1766, and staked off its location on April 12. Melchior Rasp, the mason, built the stone cellar, and Christian Triebel, the carpenter, with his apprentice Christian Strehle, built the timber frame. Rasp and Triebel had both come to North Carolina in the fall of 1755 and would later collaborate as fire wardens and builders of the waterworks. At the end of June, workers from Bethabara raised the timber walls into place, celebrating the completion of their labors with "a bit of festivity . . . several bottles of wine."[26]

This so-called First House was a one-and-one-half story structure, 38 feet long and 26 feet wide, with a stone cellar, a brick chimney and, like most of the other early Moravian buildings, a tile roof. The spaces between the braces and uprights of its oak frame were filled with wooden lath wrapped with straw and clay. (In the summer of 1766, Joseph Muller made the first bricks at Salem, so that the walls of later houses could be filled with bricks.) Though the interior was plastered, the structural posts and beams of the frame projected from the walls and ceiling. (This is evidenced by a 1798 suggestion that the exposed beams in the old frame houses should be painted with a mixture of unslaked lime and milk to improve their appearance.) In May, 1766, the authorities decided to make the windows of this First House three panes high and three panes wide. In July, the First House was so far completed that part of its first story could be used as a temporary meeting hall. In October, prefabricated doors and windows, complete with casings and glass, were carried from Bethabara, where they had been made, to Salem.

In July, 1766, Brother Reuter drew the plan for a second timber-framed house, a two-story structure. Since the meeting hall in the First House was too small, the partitions in the first story of this Second House were left out, so that it could be used as a new gathering place for the people. (Later it would be used as the town store.) Because of a shortage of workmen, construction of the Second House could not proceed until the First House had been nearly completed. Matthew Schropp complained in October, 1766, when the cornerstone of the Second House was laid: "How embarrassed I am at times for a couple of reliable masons and helpers and carpenters, so that Salem can be advanced! With strangers nothing can be accomplished here. They come for a week, fill their belly and are gone."[27]

A Third House was staked off in February, 1767, its foundation laid in March, the frame raised in May, and nearly completed in July. The Fourth House, now the oldest surviving building at Salem, was begun in July, 1767, the timber frame was raised in November and the house was completed in early 1768. The Third and Fourth Houses had similar, but reversed, plans, a timber frame with brick nogging and, like many other early buildings, tile-covered roofs with flaring eaves. After Brother Marshall first visited the new town in February 1768, he reported: "In Salem I find three family houses ready for use, all made of framework covered with clay, or framework filled with brick and clay. All are one story,

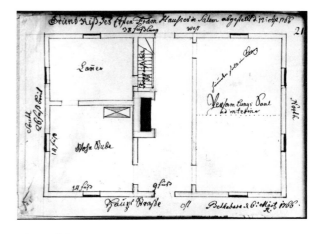

Plan of the First House, Salem, 1766.
Archiv, Herrnhut

The Fourth House, Salem, 1767–68.

with two rooms, a kitchen and a cellar. In addition there is one two-story house [with] a small congregation hall below and above two rooms and a kitchen."[28]

Frederick William Marshall drew the plan of the Single Brothers House, residence and workshop for the unmarried men of the town, in June, 1768. The foundation stone was laid on the northwest corner of the square in August, but it was not until May, 1769, that the framing was completed with help of men from Bethabara and Bethania, who celebrated by blowing trumpets from the top of the building. The Single Brothers House is a two-story half-timber structure with a fieldstone cellar, tall attic and tile roof. The spaces between the braces and studs of its massive oak frame are filled with brick. Although the Moravians now had plenty of brick, they still had only a limited supply of the lime which was so essential for preparing mortar for brick and stone walls. (Sometimes they could get lime only by bringing wagonloads of oyster shells two hundred miles from the coast.) A pent eave, supported by extensions of the second-story floor joists, helped protect the brick nogging, which had been laid up with little or no lime, from damage by rainwater. Wooden gutters, made from logs split in half and hollowed through the center, protected the walls from rain and collected water for cisterns.

In December, 1769, the Single Brothers House was dedicated. A kitchen and weaving room were in the cellar; a small assembly hall and living rooms were in the first story; and a sleeping hall for forty men and a sick room were in the second story. In 1771 a log workshop, sketched by Brother Muschbach, who was the steward of the single brothers, was built behind the original house. In 1786 a brick wing was added at the southern end of the original house, containing more sleeping rooms, a new kitchen, meeting hall and dining room. In March, while some of the single brothers were digging the cellar for this addition, the sides of their excavation collapsed, burying two men and killing one of them. In June, 1786, the first lightning rod in Salem was installed at the Single Brothers House. In 1800, when the supply of lime had finally become more plentiful, the pent eave was removed and the exterior was plastered. Today the exterior has been restored to its original appearance, and the log workshop, demolished in 1921, has been reconstructed.

While the Single Brothers House was being built, most of the Moravians remained at Bethabara. They could not come to Salem until a larger meeting hall for the people, who had continued to gather in the Second House, and rooms for church officials and the single women could be built. In May, 1769, Brother Marshall presented his plan for a Congregation House which was to be built on the northeast corner of

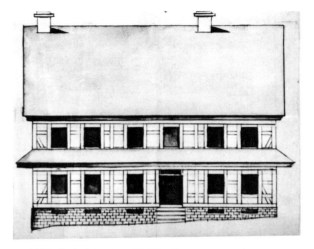

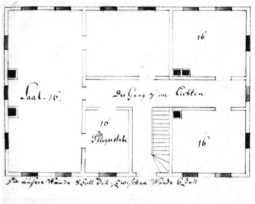

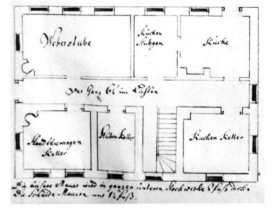

Elevation and plan of the Single Brothers House, Salem, 1768. *Archiv, Herrnhut*

Single Brothers House, Salem, 1768–69.

the square. The authorities, at that time still troubled by the short supply of lime, faced a familiar problem: "To build entirely of wood is not so desirable and durable, especially in the lower story; on the other hand, to build of stone in the second story without mortar is not to be risked."[29] Therefore, the builders decided to make the cellar and first story of the Congregation House of stone, the second story and attic of half-timber with brick nogging. Rocks for the lower walls were brought from the banks of Peter's Creek, laid up with clay and then covered with plaster. There were wooden steps, later replaced with stone, wooden gutters, a tile roof and first-story pent eave. Between March and June, 1771, the garden was fenced and planted with peas, spinach, lettuce, radishes, corn, potatoes and turnips.

The Congregation House was dedicated in November, 1771. In February of the following year, four single sisters from Bethabara came to live in the south end of the building. In April, Marshall and his wife, later joined by other Church officials and two widowers, moved into the north end. In October, an organ was installed in a new congregation hall at the center of the second story. A 1776 inventory indicates that at that time an attic room, containing four beds, was used to lodge travellers. The congregation hall on the second story contained the organ, a table for ministers draped with green cloth and black leather, more than twelve benches, two brass chandeliers, stoves, seven metal wall sconces and offering boxes for the poor. In September, 1794, the first-story pent eave was removed and the exterior plastered. The Congregation House was demolished in 1854, when a new building for Salem Female Academy was built on the site.

When the Congregation House was completed, most of the residents of Bethabara finally moved to Salem and the authorities, concerned about the risk of fire, began to plan a town waterworks. Water would be led from springs on the northwest side of town and then down the hill to buildings around the square. (A drawing attributed to Frederick William Marshall is a study of ground levels for this gravity-fed system and also indicates that he wanted to build a two-story, half-timbered Store on the southwest corner of the square, as he wrote elsewhere, "to keep the plan symmetrical." The Store, finally completed in May, 1775, after a long disagreement between Marshall and the storekeeper, Traugott Bagge, was a one-and-one-half-story stone building.) In 1777 Brothers Triebel and Krause were put in charge of building the waterworks. The spring was enclosed with a well house "so that the crawfish cannot get in." Wooden pipes, made of oak logs ten to twelve feet long, with holes bored through their center, were pinned together with iron collars. The

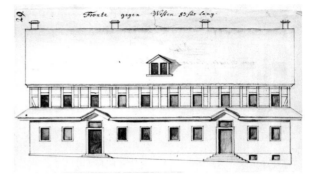

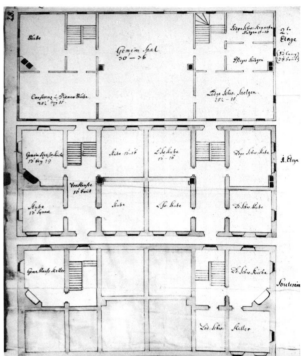

Elevation and plan of the Congregation House, Salem, 1769. *Archiv, Herrnhut*

water was led to the old Hide House, into the square, then to the rear of the Congregation House, to the Single Brothers House and to the tavern. Though the waterworks system was long plagued with difficulties and the pipes often leaked and froze, it was nevertheless a pioneering example of public planning in frontier America.

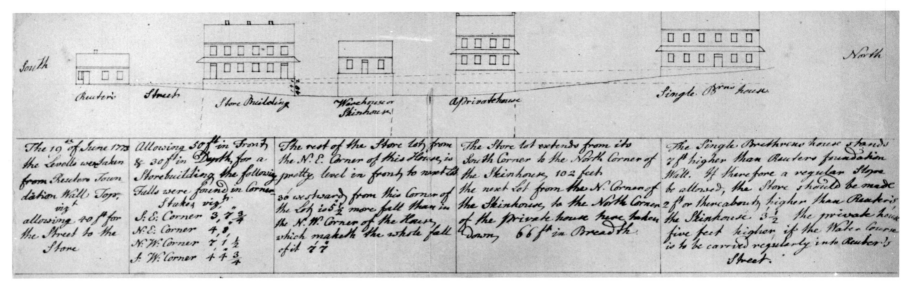

Study for waterworks, Salem, 1773. *Moravian Archives, Moravian Church in America, Southern Province*

In 1783 the thirty-six single women at Salem were still living in cramped quarters in the south end of the Congregation House. Plans for a new Single Sisters House were approved in the fall of 1783. Since lime was now more plentiful, this was to be Salem's first brick building. (No half-timbered structures were built in Salem after the Revolution. The brick buildings had entrance hoods instead of pent eaves. The exteriors of early buildings were remodeled when lime became available.) Bricks were being burned and locks and glass had been ordered from England when, in December, the Salem tavern—a half-timbered structure designed by Brother Marshall and built in 1772—burned. The tavern was so vital and so large a building project that, in January, 1784, the authorities decided to use the materials collected for the Single Sisters House to build a new tavern. So it was not until February, 1785, more than a year later, that work on the Single Sisters House could be resumed, under the supervision of Johann Gottlob Krause. In March, the cornerstone was laid. In August, the roof was raised into place, while trombones were played from the highest beam. In April, 1786, the Single Sisters House was dedicated. Like the tavern, the Single Sisters House was brick construction. Windows and doors were set under shallow segmental relieving arches. In 1812 dormers were inserted into the roof, and in 1819 an addition was made at the south end.

Single Sisters House, Salem, 1784–86.

Church, Bethabara, 1787–88.

Construction of the Single Sisters House was supervised by Johann Gottlob Krause, the potter, brick-maker and mason. His parents had come from Germany to Pennsylvania in 1744 and made their way to North Carolina in 1755, where Krause was born five years later. By 1781 Krause was established as a brick-maker and mason at Salem. Talented and high-spirited, Krause chafed under the Moravians' disciplined rules, and he was frequently in trouble for flouting the regulations—buying a slave, brawling in public, giving his laborers brandy, selling horses and rum, keeping a cow, pet dogs and cats. He was summoned before the Board of Overseers and warned to obey the rules. Finally, in 1789, Krause was told to leave Salem. He moved to Bethabara and set up a pottery in a small brick house which had been built in 1782 for a dyer, Johannes Schaub. Krause died in 1802.

Meanwhile, a new Church was needed for the families still living at Bethabara, and Frederick Marshall provided the design for it in 1787.[30] Abraham Loesch, a mason from Salem, supervised the quarrying of stone and building of walls. In February and March, the stone and lumber were prepared and the cellar built. In April, May and June, the exterior stone walls and interior brick partitions were laid. The shingled roof was finished in July, the tower was in place at the end of August. In October, the interior was plastered, three tile stoves were installed and window sash were put into place. In November, 1788, the Church was dedicated. Minister's quarters are part of the Church, with a separate, lower gable roof. The stone walls and brick gables have been plastered and pencilled to simulate ashlar. Even before its restoration in 1969–70, the Bethabara Church was one of the best preserved of all Moravian buildings in North Carolina.

Though Johann Krause had been expelled from Salem, his talents were needed there. In 1784 Brother Marshall had complained: "We are handicapped by lack of workmen. Our master carpenter, Triebel, is in his seventieth year, and our master mason, Melchior Rasp, is in his sixty-eighth year, and both are in the sick-room."[31] In 1791 he again wrote: "At present we have neither master carpenter nor master mason nor brick-maker, and so cannot think of any extensive building project."[32] So, when the authorities approved plans for a Boys School in 1793, they had to call on Krause to supervise it, though most of the actual work was done by outside laborers. In February, 1794, Krause agreed to supervise "all the work of masonry in stone and brick, wattle and daub plastering and white-washing the entire house, to plaster and smooth the outside walls, to cover the roof, to pave the hall and lower parts, to make and overlay cellar vault, chimneys and fireplaces." He

Church, Bethabara, drawing by Julius Mickey, 1846. *Wachovia Historical Society*

Boys School, Salem, 1794. Top: Sketch by Nathanael Schober, 1798. *Moravian Archives, Southern Province.* Bottom: Rear view of Boys School, a 19th-century photograph. *Old Salem*

would begin work after Easter, hire workmen and "give them the usual drams." (Records indicate that Krause purchased eleven gallons of brandy for his workmen.) Construction began in April, 1794, and the school was occupied by twenty-eight pupils, ten of whom were boarders, in December, 1794. The elevated basement was stone, laid up in clay and protected by a coat of plaster; the main story and gables were brick, laid in Flemish bond with stringcourse and a decorative design on the west gable. The first story contained a living room, bedroom and kitchen for the teachers; the second story contained four school rooms; and the attic had a sleeping hall for the boys. A drawing indicates that open sheds were to stand in the yard behind the school for outdoor recreation.

In October, 1794, Christoph Vogler, the village gunsmith who had come to North Carolina from Maine as a child, petitioned to build a house in Salem. When he asked to have a timber-frame building with a shingle roof, the authorities told him to build a stone house with a tile roof. In January, 1797, Vogler proposed to build a stone house with a stone cellar, half-timber upper story and a tile roof. Finally, he decided to have Johann Krause build a brick house with a tile roof. Vogler would use the north end as his shop and forge and the south end as his dwelling. Krause laid the walls in Flemish bond, over a stone foundation, with moulded brick watertable and windows set under shallow relieving arches, and put his initials in the south gable. The house was built between February and December, 1797. In 1870 a later owner, Francis Meller, demolished one chimney and rebuilt it to serve as a bake oven for his confectionary shop and added walls, fireplaces, a new stair, a second story and more and larger windows. The present appearance of the Christoph Vogler House, though essentially accurate, is the result of considerable restoration.

In April, 1797, Frederick Marshall drew plans for the Church at Salem.[33] This was the most important of all the public buildings but it was the last to be built. In May, 1798, ground was broken for the Church just beyond the northeast corner of the square. Following instructions from the congregation, Marshall faced the gable of the Church forward, rather than parallel to the street like all the other buildings of Salem. The brick walls were laid in Flemish bond with moulded watertable, stringcourse and stone sills. In September, the timbers of the roof were raised into place. Roof tiles were burned by the aged Johann Gottlob Krause, but they were too soft and had to be replaced in 1803 with wooden shingles of yellow poplar, painted red to simulate the appearance of tiles. The steeple was covered with tin and painted Brunswick green. Copper gutters, also painted green, were

Boys School, stair. *Frances Benjamin Johnston, Library of Congress*

Christoph Vogler House, Salem, 1797.

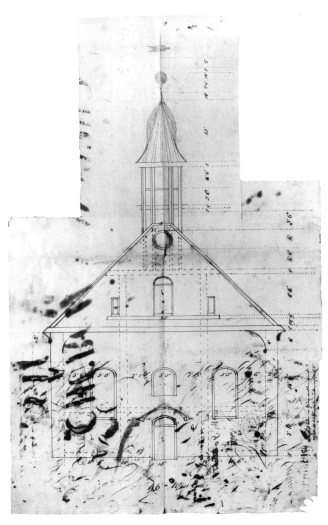

Church, Salem, 1798–1800, with Frederick Marshall's drawing for its design.
Drawing from Moravian Archives, Southern Province

Dr. Samuel Vierling House, Salem, 1801–02.

made by Christoph Vogler, the village gunsmith.[34] (This is the first recorded use of metal gutters in Salem.) The bell and a golden weather-vane were made in Pennsylvania. The carpenters were three members of the Wolff family, Lutherans who lived near Bethania. Chandeliers were painted cobalt blue, the candle holders were painted yellow. The door and window frames, galleries and steeple were painted light yellow. Bricks around windows and doors were painted bright red. The Church was dedicated in November, 1800. The interior was remodelled in 1870 and 1913.

Up the street from the Church, on the site of Widow Yarrell's orchard, Johann Krause built a two-story brick house for Dr. Samuel Vierling. Born in Silesia in 1765, Vierling had come to Salem in 1790 to be the town doctor. The plan was presented to the authorities in March, 1801, the foundation work began in May, and Dr. Vierling moved into the house in June, 1802. As usual, Krause embellished the gable end with decorative patterns of brickwork. Like the Church, the bricks 'round the door and windows were painted bright red. The house had wooden gutters, which continued to be used in Salem as late as 1821. Dr. Vierling's house was the last of Brother Krause's works in Salem, for he died in 1802.

In late 1802 the officials of Salem decided to open a Girls School, principally for non-Moravians from outside the town. In February, 1803, a plan was approved for a two-story building, to accommodate sixty girls and a few teachers, to be built on the east side of the square. The plan was made by John Gambold, who had come to North Carolina from Pennsylvania in 1791 and who was for seven years steward of the single brothers. After Krause's death, roof tiles were in short supply, so the roof was made with wooden shingles painted red. In August, 1803, the site was cleared, the building staked off and the cellar dug. In October, the cornerstone was laid. In February, 1804, after Gambold left Salem, Frederick Meinung was given charge of construction. Meinung, a surveyor like his father, had been born at Salem in 1782. He was also employed copying music, cutting gravestone inscriptions, singing and teaching the violin. In May, 1804, the cellar walls were completed, the first floor joists were laid and the brick walls of the first story were commenced. A year later, it was still not decided whether to make the windows "up & down, English style, or casement, German style."[35] In July, 1805, the school was occupied. In 1824 an addition was made to the north end, and in 1837 a clerestory was added to the roof. In 1873 the school was further enlarged, but it has now been restored to its 1837 appearance. Windows and doors were decorated with painted bricks.

Girls School, Salem, 1803–05, its original design and a mid-19th-century lithograph by P. S. Duval of Philadelphia, showing additions made in 1824 and 1837. *Drawing from Moravian Archives, Southern Province, Lithograph from North Carolina Archives and History.*

Two views of Salem, paintings by Daniel Welfare, 1824. *Wachovia Historical Society*

In August, 1823, L. Newby of Fayetteville visited Salem and observed: "On my arrival here, I found myself in a scene entirely new—a pretty little Dutch town, with the houses built somewhat in the Dutch style—the streets pav'd & a large Church with a Clock in it which was striking the hour of nine as I pass'd it. Such a scene in the back part of North Carolina must strike a person . . . with wonder!"[36] About two-hundred and fifty people lived at Salem in the early 19th century, one-fifth of the Moravians in North Carolina. It had taken nearly a half century for them to build their amazing little city in the wilderness. The unity of the Moravian community, inspired by adversity in Europe, had been strengthened by hardship and isolation in America. After the Revolution, the authorities began to complain about a "dangerous . . . spirit of American freedom" spreading among the Moravians.[37] More and more young people, less and less willing to obey the rules, were sent away from Salem or decided to leave. Adoption of building regulations in 1788 was a signal that the old conventions of building were being abandoned. Frederick William Marshall, Administrator of Wachovia for forty years, died in 1802. Now there were more traders and travellers coming to Salem to buy Moravian pottery, cloth and furniture. In 1849 a new town of Winston was founded near Salem and soon engulfed the old Moravian community. But today the Church bell still rings above the beautifully restored buildings, many of them open to the public, around the square at Salem.

One of the nearest and friendliest of the Moravians' neighbors was Adam Spach, a settler who lived just beyond the southern boundary of their Wachovia tract.[38] Born in Lower Alsace in 1720, the son of a weaver, Spach came to America at the age of thirteen. After serving his six-year term as an indentured servant in Maryland, he married and moved to North Carolina in 1753. During the French and Indian War he took refuge with the Moravians at Bethabara, and in 1770 he joined the Moravian church and became steward of their South Fork Society, an early settlement of about fifteen families, later called Friedberg. There, between May and December, 1774, he built a rock house on a hillside over a spring. The house has been destroyed. Though the exterior walls were stone, the interior walls and partitions as well as arches over windows and door openings were brick.

Before the Revolution, perhaps one-third of Pennsylvania's population was of German birth or descent and about one-third of those moved to the South. In North Carolina, Germans concentrated their settlements in Rowan, Cabarrus and Mecklenberg counties, where they built notable stone structures. Michael Braun, a wheelwright born in Ger-

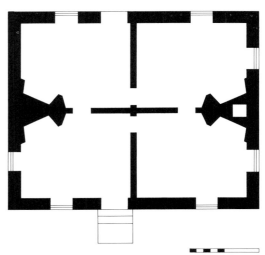

Adam Spach House, Friedberg, 1774, with its plan. *Library of Congress*

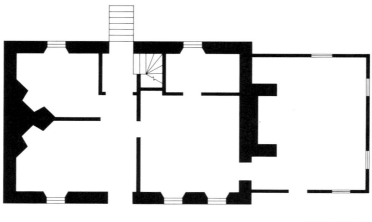

Michael Braun House, Salisbury vicinity, 1766, with its plan.

many, came to North Carolina by way of Pennsylvania. His two-story, gable-roofed stone house stands three miles outside of Salisbury. The front wall is made of carved stone, but the other walls are uncoursed fieldstone. Braun's name, with the inscription in abbreviated German, "My undertaking completed with thanks to Christ, 1766," is carved into a large stone set in the front wall between two second-story windows. To protect the foundations from rainwater, the builder made a stone watertable on the south wall and pent eaves on the north and west walls. The house has been twice restored, and the interiors are complete reconstructions. Only the walls and two window frames are original. The house is open to the public at limited times.

Hezekiah Alexander, a Scotch-Irish Presbyterian, came to Mecklenburg County sometime after 1754 from Maryland, near the Pennsylvania border.[39] Establishing himself as a blacksmith and planter, he built a stone house near a branch of Sugar Creek, located in present-day Charlotte, in 1774. The house has two-foot-thick stone walls, segmental window openings with keystones, a cypress-shingled roof and a simple four-room plan without a hallway. It is open to the public. Ezekial Wallis built another stone house, some nine miles away, about 1778. Wallis's house, demolished in the 1960's, had coursed stone walls, a gable roof and conventional three-room colonial plan, but the southeast gable had curious circular and heart-shaped openings, probably for ventilation, each surrounded by decorative stonework.

The Pennsylvania settlers of neighboring Rowan County used log churches until after the Revolution. The Lutherans began Zion Church, near Rockwell, in 1792 and completed it in 1795. Nearby, the German Reformed congregation began their own Grace Church in 1795 but did not complete it until November, 1811. Both churches are two-story stone structures, with gable roofs, segmental arches over the principal windows and stone watertables. The bell towers were added to both churches about 1900, and both have lost their original interiors. The German settlers built many log and frame structures, as well as stone houses and churches, but it is certainly evident that the best German buildings were far better than those made by settlers of English background in the North Carolina piedmont.

Outside of the German settlements, one of the most carefully built houses of the late 18th-century North Carolina frontier must have been William Lenoir's house in the vicinity of present-day Patterson in Caldwell County.[40] Lenoir was a Revolutionary soldier and state legislator who had come to North Carolina from southeastern Virginia, where he had been born in 1751. In 1782, he began to purchase land and built a

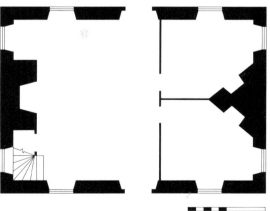

Ezekial Wallis House, Mecklenburg County, c. 1778, with its plan. *Frances Benjamin Johnston, Library of Congress*

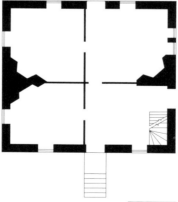

Hezekiah Alexander House, Charlotte, 1774, with its plan. *Gordon H. Schenck, Jr.*

Grace Church, Rowan County, 1795–1811, bell tower added c. 1900.
Frances Benjamin Johnston, Library of Congress

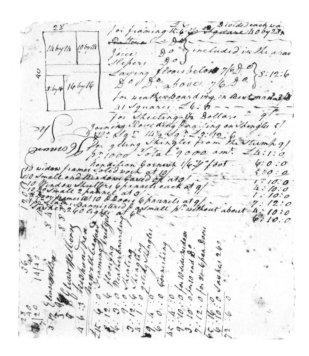

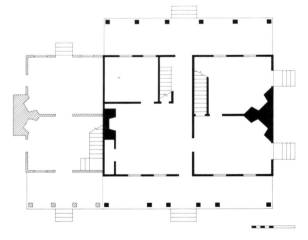

Builder's estimate for construction of William Lenoir House, Patterson vicinity, c. 1788, probably by Thomas Fields. *Lenoir Family Papers, Southern Historical Collection, University of North Carolina.*

log house near the Yadkin River, including the site of old Fort Defiance, a stockade built a few years earlier to protect frontiersmen against the Cherokee Indians. There Lenoir produced tobacco and cotton and operated grist- and sawmills, a distillery and a cotton gin. In March, 1788, a housewright named Thomas Fields was hired to build a new home, "a house Forty feet long & Twenty Eight feet wide Two Stories with four Rooms on each Story," promising to make a "Cornish . . . with Mondilions," "Stairs well Bannistered," "Wash Boards and chair-Boards . . . Round all the Rooms" and "good thick shingles from the Stump." (His building estimate, with a sketch plan, has survived among family papers.) The building was so far advanced by November, 1791, that Lenoir hired John Goldsmith to fire bricks and build chimneys. The spaces between the timbers of the walls were filled with brick nogging. The house was completed in 1792. Beaded weatherboarding was painted brown, the modillion cornice and window frames were painted green and the shutters and scallop porch trim were painted blue. Lenoir ordered looking glasses and green carpets from Scotland, and they were shipped into the frontier by way of Wilmington and Fayetteville. William Lenoir's son Thomas made additions at the west end of the house in 1822–23, after his family returned to live with his aged father. There has been considerable restoration of the elaborately panelled fireplace wall in the parlor. The house is open to the public.

Philip Alston came to Moore County from Halifax in 1772 and built a small cottage at the horseshoe bend of Deep River north of present-day Carthage.[41] Though he became a justice of the peace and clerk of court, Alston fled from North Carolina in 1790 when he was accused of murdering one man and ordering the killing of another. Eight years later, Benjamin Williams, a Revolutionary soldier, cotton planter, state legislator, Congressman and Governor, purchased Alston's house and enlarged it. In July, 1803, he described his home as "a tolerable two-Story House with the Frame now ready to put up for a Wing of 24 by 20 at each end." These wings were later demolished and were not rebuilt when the house was restored in the 1950's. The house is open to the public.

An incomplete survey of North Carolina counties made by various local citizens in 1810 gives us a vivid portrait of the state's small villages, plank roads, toll bridges, lonely forests and primitive buildings. Bartlett Yancey described Caswell County's three towns: Leasburg ("It has one Store, a grocery Shop, a Sadler's Shop, and a Cabinet-maker's Shop, with about 10 or 12 Houses"), Milton ("It has 2 Stores, a Sadler's Shop, a Hatter's Shop, a tavern with about 15 or 20 houses") and Caswell

William Lenoir House, Patterson vicinity, c. 1788–92, additions 1822–23, with its plan. Detail of panelling of fireplace wall, before restoration. *Frances Benjamin Johnston, Library of Congress*

Top: Philip Alston House, Carthage vicinity, c. 1772. Bottom: James Bryant House, Southern Pines vicinity, c. 1820.

Court House, later called Yanceyville ("It has 2 taverns, a Store, a Hatter's Shop with about 15 Houses"). William Dickson wrote of Duplin County: "The first inhabitants . . . built and lived in log cabins, and as they became more Wealthy some of them Built framed Clapboard Houses with Clay Chimneys. At Present there are many good Houses, well Constructed, with Brick Chimneys and Glass lights. There are no Stone or Brick-walled Houses, nor any that can be called Edifices in the County. The greatest number of the Citizens yet build in the old Stile." Moore County was reported to have no towns, only a village at the courthouse containing eight or ten dwellings: "The major part of our buildings are Log Houses." Alexander Sneed wrote of Rockingham County: "The buildings in this county are Generally of wood, some Framed but the greater part of hewn logs, covered with Shingles with Brick and Stone Chimneys. . . . We have a tollerable wooden Court House, painted. . . . There is but one Framed Meeting House in the County. . . . There are a great many . . . built in the most cheapest manner of hewn logs." In Wayne County, J. Slocumb reported that the largest hamlet, Waynesboro on the north bank of the Neuse River, had no more than five or six houses, a jail and a courthouse, "all of wood & Single Story except the Court House." He added, "The Houses generally throughout the County is of wood and Single Story." In 1820 only six towns in North Carolina had populations of more than one thousand people.[42]

James Bryant's house in Moore County was built about 1820 in the vicinity of present-day Southern Pines. A two-story frame structure, with exterior end chimney, gable roof, shed porch in front and shed rooms in the rear, it is a typical farmhouse of the early 19th-century Southern piedmont. The fireplace opening is supported by a wide segmental arch, the chimneypiece is embellished with crude but delightful geometric carving, and the walls and ceiling are sheathed with flush boards. The original windows were small, without glazed sash, and were closed only with wooden shutters. The house is open to the public at limited times.

Wright Tavern in Wentworth in Rockingham County is a framed, gable-roofed building which, through additions and enlargements, with an open passageway in place of an enclosed stair hall, has developed into a dogtrot plan associated with log cabins. William Wright built the early section sometime before 1814. His son James probably added the eastern end, with an open passageway and stair set under a segmental arch, with keystone and fluted pilasters, after he inherited the property in 1824. Sherill's Inn in Buncombe County, near the old stage road be-

Top: Wright Tavern, Wentworth, before 1814, additions after 1824. Bottom: Sherill's Inn, Asheville vicinity, enlargement of early log house. *Sherill's Inn photograph by Bayard Wootten from* Old Homes and Gardens of North Carolina, *with permission of its publisher,* The University of North Carolina Press.

tween Rutherford and Asheville, is also interesting because of idiosyncratic enlargements. Bedford Sherrill, opening a tavern and stagecoach stop, enlarged an earlier cabin into a long, rambling gable-roofed log and frame structure. Second-story rooms can be reached only by means of a curious stair which ascends from the outside beside the central chimney.

St. Andrew's Church, Woodleaf, was built on the main road between Mocksville and Salisbury by a carpenter named Jacob Correll in 1840. A large, barn-like, gable-roofed structure, set on a low fieldstone foundation with wood-sheathed interiors and simple benches, it is the type of simple building which must have been so typical of 19th-century North Carolina.

Frontier living conditions were not restricted to a particular place or era but shifted across the North Carolina territory from the 18th-century coast into the 19th-century interior. Most of North Carolina's houses were like those at the village of Washington described by Robert Hunter in 1786: "all of wood, without either form or regularity."[43] In 1825 Prince Bernhard of Saxe-Weimar found only two brick houses in Tarboro, a town of eight hundred people.[44] Carl Arfwedson came to North Carolina in 1832: "All the houses near the roads deserve no better name than that of huts. Built of the trunks of trees, the branches of which are not even cut off, laid loosely on the top of each other, so that the ends only join."[45] In 1840, 1844 wooden houses and only thirty-eight brick or stone houses were built in North Carolina.[46] But simple houses did not necessarily represent poverty. Sarah Williams, the young New York-born bride of a North Carolina planter, wrote in October, 1853: "Ambition is satisfied here by numbering its thousands of dollars [in] acres of land and hundreds of negroes. Houses, furniture and dress are nothing. For instance, the Dr.'s brother, a very wealthy man, lives in a brown wood house without lathing or plastering. . . . This is the common style of houses, and ours, which is finished, the exception."[47] In the same year a professor at Wake Forest College complained: "There are few things in which we are more deficient than in Architecture. The State is covered with huge squares and parallelograms of painted weatherboards."[48] Frontier living conditions—and frontier architecture—continued in most parts of interior North Carolina until after the Civil War.

St. Andrew's Church, Woodleaf, 1840.
North Carolina Archives and History

III. *The Federal Era*

In the absence of professionally trained architects, houses were planned by their owners and public buildings were planned by committees, with the assistance of joiners and housewrights. Usually, the owner or committee supplied an idea for the building's plan, giving the carpenter a sketch of their own devising, taking as a model the design from a book or another building in the neighborhood. In March, 1829, Duncan Cameron, newly elected President of the State Bank in Raleigh, conferred with builder J. H. Smith on plans for a new house and Smith then sent him "a plan . . . something like what I understood you [to want]."[1] The owner generally supplied the bricks and lumber, ordering them or having his own laborers make them. The builder was usually a carpenter or mason, but he could hire other craftsmen like plasterers, itinerant painters or carvers to finish off the interior. In April, 1803, a building committee advertised for someone to build the new academy at Wilmington: "The persons contracting to find all the labour necessary to complete the brick work, and to cover the roof with slate or tile."[2]

In 1799 John Steele, a powerful Federalist, state legislator, Congressman and famous breeder of race horses, decided to build a new house in Salisbury. Fortunately for historians, Steele was spending most of the time between 1796 and 1802 in Philadelphia and Washington, where he was Comptroller of the U.S. Treasury, and so the progress of his housebuilding was preserved in letters. Steele hired Elem Sharpe, a local housewright, to construct the frame of the dwelling and complete all its woodwork. A sketchy plan, a list of a few special requirements and a general admonition that the job was to be done "in a workmanlike manner" were all that the builder needed as a guide in early 19th-century America. The house was to be thirty-two feet square, with a conventional side-hall plan. Girders and corner posts were to be "of good sound post oak," the rest of the frame of pine. The roof was to have "a plain cheap Cornish" with pine shingles to be "rather flatter than common." The first story was to be ten feet, eight inches, between floor and ceiling, and the second story was to be nine feet, four inches, high.[3] Timber for Steele's house was cut between April and July, 1799. In March, 1800, Steele hired a plasterer from Philadelphia, John Langdon, to go to Salisbury to complete the interiors of the house.[4] Langdon reached Salisbury in mid-April—and was still in Rowan County as late as May, 1805, when he took nineteen-year-old William Adam as apprentice.[5] In August, 1801, William R. Davie ruefully congratulated Steele on his new house, "the most decent chateau in the neighborhood, enough I am afraid to mark you soon as an Aristocrat!"[6]

Before about 1840, one carpenter or mason worked with one or two apprentices and a handful of black artisans to build houses or other buildings. One survey of arts and crafts in North Carolina has recorded more than one thousand housewrights and carpenters who took apprentices between 1715 and 1840, but the careers of only a few of them are known.[7] William Good was a house carpenter in New Bern who began his career about 1765 and died in 1802 at the age of eighty-two. In Edenton, George Morgan was active at least between 1784 and 1797 before his death in 1810. John Dewey of New Bern was active between at least 1789 and 1817. Benjamin Good, one of Dewey's apprentices, was active between 1796 and 1812. In the Charlotte area, William Flinn was apprenticed as a house carpenter and joiner in 1789 at the age of eighteen and worked at least for another twenty years. William Jones of Franklin County was apprenticed in 1805 and continued in the building trade until his death in the 1850's. Elias Fort of Hillsborough was active between 1812 and 1818 at the least. In 1816, Fort tried to organize the carpenters and house-joiners, his "brother mechanicks," to establish standards for work and uniform prices.[8] In September, 1810, a mason, Henry Gorman, complained that his nineteen-year-old apprentice William Hollyman had run off with some plastering tools and a small, shaggy-haired, brown-and-white-spotted dog named Ask-Him. "I will give Two Dollars for my tools, twenty-five cents for Ask'm and," Gorman added resentfully, "ten cents for William!"[9]

In the introduction to his *American Builder's Companion* of 1806, Asher Benjamin, the Massachusetts housewright who, despite his lack of sophisticated training, became the most important American architectural writer of the early 19th century, wrote: "Old-fashioned workmen, who have for many years followed the footsteps of Palladio and Langley, will no doubt leave their old path with great reluctance." Inevitably, those who had worked their way from apprentice to house carpenter to builder, trained by experience and tradition instead of academic study, would be conservative. Reliance on books, most of

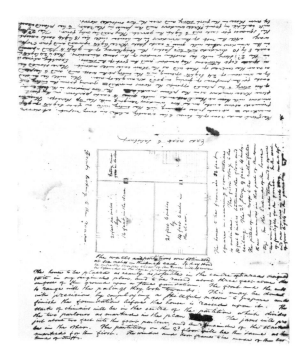

Elem Sharpe's agreement to build John Steele's house at Salisbury in 1799. *John Steele Papers, Southern Historical Collection, University of North Carolina*

which were published in 18th-century England, or American imprints copied from them, further encouraged this architectural conservatism. Francis Price's *The British Carpenter*, originally published in London in 1733, and Batty Langley's *The Builder's Jewel*, first issued in London in 1741, were offered for sale in Fayetteville in September, 1790, and *The Builder's Jewel* was offered for sale at Edenton as late as March, 1808.[10]

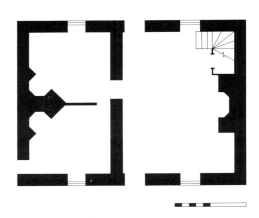

John Haley House, East Lexington Avenue, High Point, 1786.

John Haley's house, at the corner of East Lexington Avenue and McGuinn Avenue in High Point, was built in 1786 for a Quaker settler who had come to the area some twenty years earlier.[11] Haley was a blacksmith, local sheriff and road commissioner. His house faced the main road between Salisbury and Petersburg, and, after Haley died in 1813, the building became a popular stagecoach stop. The three-room plan and Flemish bond walls of Haley's house continue colonial traditions. Unfortunately, the building had been badly "restored" in the 1940's, destroying much of the original interior. When more careful restoration began a generation later, the interior had to be mostly re-created. The stair was rebuilt in its original location at the northeast corner of the main room, a one-inch board wall between the two smaller chambers was rebuilt, windows were reconstructed using a 19th-century photograph as a guide, and virtually all of the interior trim and hardware are conjectural recreations. The house is open to the public. Matthew Moore's house in the vicinity of Danbury, overlooking the Dan River Valley, is the oldest structure in Stokes County. Built in the same year, it is strikingly similar to Haley's house, a one-and-one-half story brick structure with Flemish bond walls, gable roof, segmental window arches and a three-room plan.

In 1785, Patty Person, the rich and strong-willed sister of Thomas Person, a North Carolina surveyor and land speculator, married Major Francis Taylor, a Virginian who had served as aid to Nathaniel Greene during the Revolution. It is believed that Patty Person Taylor built her house, near present-day Louisburg in Franklin County, sometime between 1783, when she took possession of the property, and 1785, when she married. Her house is a two-story frame structure, with a gable roof, exterior end chimneys, a tall brick and fieldstone foundation, a central hall plan and one-story rear wing. The interior is finished with a simple flush board ceiling, wooden cornice and plaster walls above panelled wainscot. An unidentified carpenter, perhaps the same one who worked at Prestwould in Mecklenburg County, Virginia, installed a handsome stair, with wide, flat handrail and turned balusters, and commanding chimneypieces, with pulvinated frieze, Greek fret, dentils and projecting corner blocks. The same anonymous craftsman was probably responsible for the nearly identical late Georgian stair and mantel at the so-called Boley Hunt House, photographed in the late 1930's. This house, once located in Vance County, next to Franklin County, is otherwise unknown today. This same workman may also have done the mantels at the so-called Foster House just east of Ingleside in Franklin County. Yet undocumented, this house would seem to date from the 1780's. A two-story frame building, on a low fieldstone foundation, with exterior brick end chimneys and gable roof, the Foster House has a simple two-room plan. The larger room, part of which is now partitioned to form a hall, has panelled wainscot, dentil cornice and a magnificent panelled overmantel flanked by fluted pilasters on pedestals.

In 1792 the State of North Carolina purchased part of Joel Lane's farm outside the village of Bloomsbury and laid out the new city of Raleigh as the state capital. Rodham Atkins, a builder who had come to North Carolina from Massachusetts as early as 1790, when he took Ephraim Rogers, an orphan, to be his apprentice in the carpenter's and joiner's trade, supervised construction of the State House between 1792 and 1796. (It is interesting to note that another New Englander, a "Major Calder, Architect and practical builder of Washington, originally of Boston," was contractor for the new Governor's House in 1814–15.)[12] The builder's agreement specified that the brick State House was to have foundations four feet wide, pine floors, a hipped roof covered with shingles ("well painted with some lively colours") and four chimneys.

Chimneypieces at Patty Person Taylor House, Louisburg vicinity, c. 1783–85, and Boley Hunt House, Vance County, undocumented. *Boley Hunt photograph by Frances Benjamin Johnston, Library of Congress*

Chimneypieces at Patty Person Taylor House, c. 1783–85, and Foster House,
Ingleside vicinity, undocumented.

The Senate and Commoners' Hall were to be "wainscotted 4 feet high with modillion cornish, the other 4 smaller Rooms with chair & wash boards only & all the rooms completely plastered & painted of various colours," with galleries over the legislative chambers. The builder was to install two armchairs for the speakers and large brass locks on all the doors.[13] By August, 1793, bricks were being made in five kilns, the walls had been raised about ten feet above the ground and all the doors and windows of the lower story were in place.[14]

The State House, a two-and-one-half story structure with a tall hipped roof and pedimented central pavilion, was old-fashioned even when new, for it was much like the provincial Palladian public buildings erected in other colonies before the Revolution. The state legislature instructed the builder to make a projecting central pavilion for the State House like the one at the old Governor's Palace at New Bern. (The South Building at the University of North Carolina, begun 1798, and the Academy at Wilmington, 1803, were other large brick buildings with Palladian-inspired projecting central pavilions.) A visitor of 1798 called the new State House "a clumsy brick building, built without any regular design of architecture and totally devoid of taste or elegance."[15] William Jones, a local carpenter, added a cupola decorated with "Chinese work" to the State House in 1810,[16] the year before a watercolor view of the east end of the building was made by J. S. Glennie. The State House was remodelled in the early 1820's and burned in 1831.

In 1789 a state university had been established by the legislature, and in 1792 its building committee selected a site on a wooded hillside near an old Anglican chapel in Orange County, which soon became the village of Chapel Hill. In July, 1793, the committee hired James Patterson, a planter from Chatham County without known experience as a builder, to construct the first hall, now called Old East, a two-story, gable-roofed brick building with exterior walls two bricks thick, eight rooms on each floor, plaster walls, closets and a "Stair Case to be quite plain [with] pine handrails & square Bannisters." The University opened in February, 1795, still surrounded by rubbish, holes and brickbats left from the incomplete construction and troubled by misunderstandings between the building committee and builder.[17] Six months later Patterson complained: "When I undertook this building I thought I had to Do with a Set [of] gentlemen that would Not Quible about triffles. . . . I Have been Severely Handled by ill-Grounded suspitions that I would Not finish. . . . I was Kept and Delayed for want of bricks upwards of two Months and all Hands idle when the Dayes were Long and the weather Good. . . . I have been Keppt out of the Second Payment Nearly three

State House, Raleigh, drawing by J. S. Glennie, 1811. *Andre deCoppet Collection, Princeton University Library.*

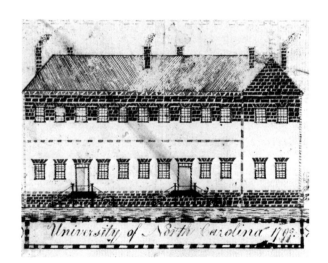

Old East, University of North Carolina, Chapel Hill, 1793–95, drawing by John Pettigrew, 1797. *Southern Historical Collection, University of North Carolina*

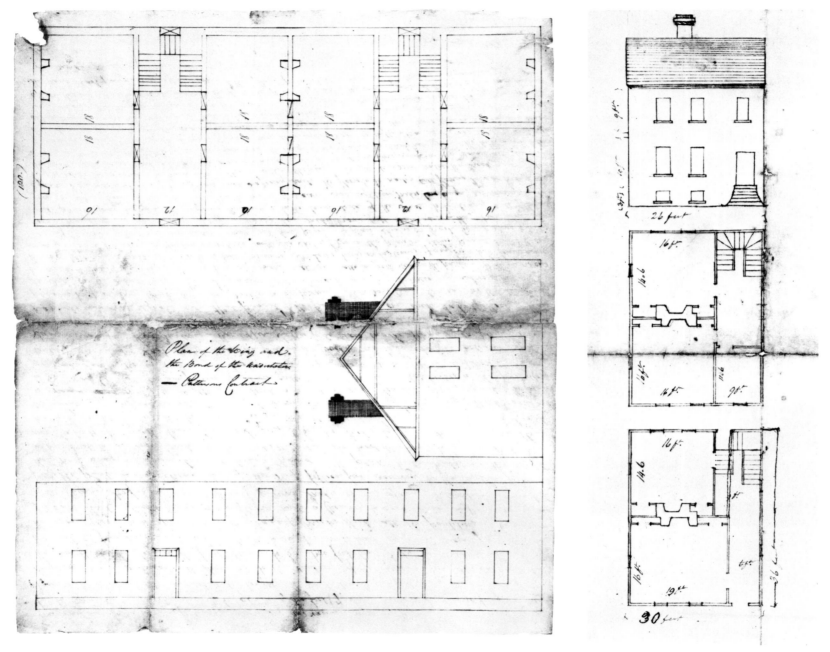

Builder's drawings for Old East and President's House, University of North Carolina, Chapel Hill, c. 1793–95. *North Carolina Collection, University of North Carolina*

Months after it was Due. . . . And Now when finished for several months No payment Can be had. . . . I am Confident that No other Person besides myself would have taken the Same Pains. . . . To be Kept out of this Last Payment so Long . . . not only Hurts My Credit but my feelings!"[18] In 1794 Samuel Hopkins, a more experienced builder from Virginia, had been hired to construct the President's House, completed in 1795.[19] By 1798 Hopkins was made superintendent of all building at the University. A South Building was begun in that year but left incomplete so long that the Trustees had to cover the unroofed shell with rough boards to protect the walls from the rain, and students, who had been crowded into the East Building, began to camp out in the incomplete South Building. Work on the South Building was not resumed until 1812 and completed in 1814.

Richard Bennehan House, Stagville, early house enlarged c. 1787.

In 1799, Richard Bennehan enlarged a small frame cottage, probably built in the late 1770's, at Stagville, north of Durham. Bennehan was born in Virginia in 1743 and apprenticed to a storekeeper in the 1760's. In 1769 he moved to North Carolina, operating a store on the road between Petersburg and Salisbury. Five years later, Bennehan moved to Stagville, purchasing the house and store of Thomas Stag in February, 1787. In 1800 Bennehan owned more than four thousand acres of land and forty-four slaves. In 1816 he described his house as "32 feet long, 22 wide, two stories, a Wing annexed, one story 24 feet by 16, with a shed

James Latta House, Huntersville vicinity, 1799.

adjg the Wing 10 feet wide, passage 12 feet."[20] The fireplace wall is embellished with tiers of panels. In 1799, another frontier merchant, James Latta, began construction of his house near the Catawba River of Mecklenburg County, near Huntersville. Latta had come to America from Ireland about 1785. His house is notable for its side-hall plan, an urban type unexpected in this rural setting, and for the richness of its interior detail, which local tradition says was carved by Hessian artisans who had remained in North Carolina after the Revolution. The walls are finished with horizontal flush boards, upon which decorative pilasters, pediments and panels have been applied. Both of these buildings are open to the public.

Oak Lawn, Benjamin Davidson House, Mecklenburg County, before 1818, seen in an early photograph prior to modern improvements. *North Carolina Archives and History*

One talented builder seems to have been responsible for two virtually identical houses, also in Mecklenburg County. Holly Bend was built for Robert Davidson, a planter, in the late 1790's on a bend of the Catawba River near Rural Hill, once overgrown with holly trees. Oak Lawn, the home of Benjamin Davidson, was probably built about the same time, although we can only say for certain that it was finished sometime before 1818. Both houses are two-and-one-half story, gable-roofed, frame structures, on low fieldstone foundations, with exterior end chimneys laid in Flemish bond and rear kitchen wings. At both houses, front doors are flanked by fluted pilasters and fluted scroll consoles. Both stairs are old-fashioned Georgian designs, with wide, flat handrails and curiously

Holly Bend, Robert Davidson House, Mecklenburg County, c. 1795. Opposite: *photograph by Frances Benjamin Johnston, from* The Early Architecture of North Carolina, *with the permission of its publisher, The University of North Carolina Press.* This page: *photographs by Frances Benjamin Johnston, Library of Congress.*

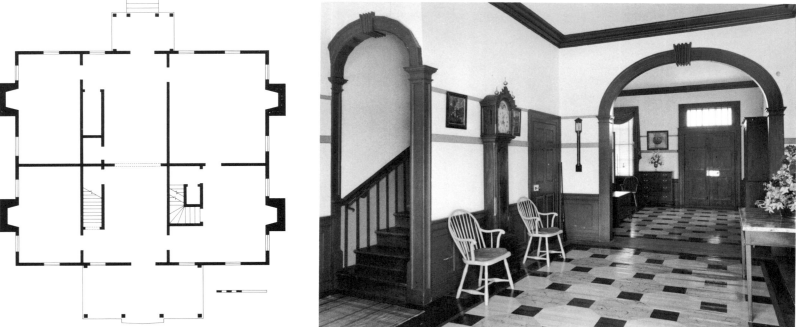

Hope Plantation, David Stone House, Windsor vicinity, with its plan and entrance hall.

short turned balusters. The interior walls and ceilings are sheathed with flush boards with a chairrail and simple wooden cornice. The doors and panelled overmantels are surmounted with entablatures, fluted consoles, broken pediments and urns, all applied over the flush boards of the walls. The right-front room at Holly Bend has a Georgian "landskip" panel (so named because it was originally intended to frame a landscape painting) with projecting corner blocks. At Oak Lawn, one upstairs room is papered with views of Captain Cook's voyages, published by Dufour at Paris in 1804 and sold at Raleigh in 1819.

The handsome house at Hope Plantation, near Windsor, was built in 1803 for David Stone. The son of a settler who had come to North Carolina from Massachusetts sometime before 1769, Stone was educated at Princeton and became a lawyer, cotton planter, state legislator, judge, congressman, senator and governor. He owned a large library, which included Abraham Swan's *British Architect*, whose Plate XLI, showing "the most convenient Situation of the Stair-Case," may have been used as the model for its plan.[21] Hope Plantation is open to the public.

Eighteenth-century English architectural traditions, though probably not a specific publication, also inspired North Carolina builders to create a distinctive group of more than twenty Palladian farm houses during the Federal era. Typically, each of these houses had a two-story central block, with its gable end facing forward to form a temple-like pediment, flanked by one-story wings. Each has a T-shaped plan with a wide hall across the front of the central block and a stair tucked into a corner of this hall. The James Semple House at Williamsburg, probably built in 1782, is an early and well-known example of this type. One of North Carolina's early examples, The Grove, was built for Willie Jones at Halifax in the 1770's. Thomas Jefferson, the possible architect of Williamsburg's Semple House, knew Willie Jones, at a time when there was much commerce between Halifax, for a few years the political center of North Carolina, and Virginia, and Jones's daughter later married Jefferson's former son-in-law John Eppes. But it would be too simple to assume that the Semple House became the progenitor for so many similar houses of the late 18th and early 19th centuries in lower Virginia and upper North Carolina.

More probably, all of these houses share the general inspiration of the monumental, temple-like compositions of English Palladianism. Robert Morris's *Select Architecture*, issued in 1757, one of the most important English architectural books, was only one of many works which illustrated temple-like houses with wings. William Halfpenny, another pop-

Palladian houses illustrated in William Halfpenny's *Useful Architecture* (London, 1752) and Robert Morris's *Select Architecture* (London, 1757). *Avery Library*

The Hermitage, John Burgwin House, Wilmington vicinity, after 1753, a late 19th-century view. *North Carolina Collection, University of North Carolina*

Undocumented house, Halifax. *North Carolina Collection, University of North Carolina*

ularizer of Palladian design whose books were intended especially for more modest builders and whose simpler designs would have been more practical for North Carolina, illustrated many small farm buildings with temple-like centers and low wings in his *Useful Architecture* of 1752. The greatest advantages of this architectural design were that it afforded grandeur on a small scale and cross-ventilation and natural light in three first-story rooms. The greatest disadvantages were that the plan did not allow for a formal stair (the Palladian originals which inspired the design generally had no second story in the main block and needed no stair) and the building could not be enlarged without sacrificing the balanced composition (a few houses which tried to widen the main block or deepen the wings are graceless).[22]

Perhaps the earliest house of this type in North Carolina—and one that probably predates the Semple House—was The Hermitage, eight miles outside of Wilmington, facing Prince George's Creek.[23] It was built shortly before the Revolution for John Burgwin, the English-born lawyer, merchant and colonial official who had come to North Carolina by way of Charleston, South Carolina, a city rich with English commerce and culture, about 1750. Receiving The Hermitage from his wife upon their marriage in 1753, Burgwin enlarged the old house already on the property. Eliza Clitherall, his daughter, recorded that "an English architect" supervised the work. In 1801 she described the house, which was 120 feet long, with a stone cellar and seventeen rooms, some of them elaborately panelled: "The Centre building was considerably higher than the wings; of two stories high and a garret. The lower story contain'd the drawing room, a large handsomely finish'd room. . . . On either side of this room were glass doors opening upon the Piazza to each wing and two other doors led to the Entry, communicating with the wings and the stair case, leading to the rooms above." There was a breakfast parlor in the south wing and a "long hall" in the north wing. "The gardens," Eliza wrote, "were large and laid out in the English style. . . . In this garden were several alcoves, summer houses, a hot-house, an octagon summer house and a gardener's tool house beneath, a fish-pond communicating with the creek. . . . Upon a mound of considerable height was erected a Brick room, containing shelves and a large number of books, chairs and table."[24] This library also contained marble busts of the Romans Marcus Aurelius, Caracalla and Faustina. Unlike most later examples, the center of The Hermitage had a hipped rather than a gable roof, and its exterior was finished with cypress shingles instead of pine weatherboards. The Hermitage burned in 1881. The only other known example with a hipped roof was an undocumented, now demolished,

Top: William Bethel House, Rockingham County, c. 1790. Bottom: Solomon Graves House, Yanceyville, c. 1790. *North Carolina Collection, University of North Carolina*

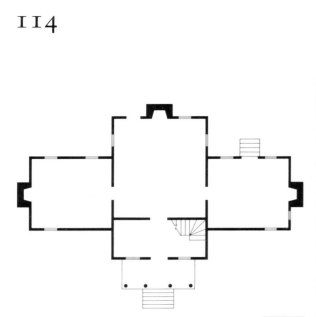

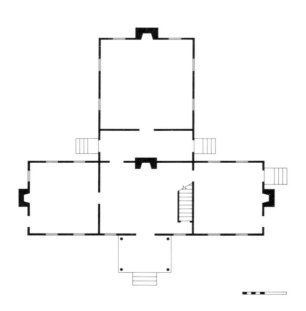

Top: Harris Place, Halifax, undocumented, with its plan. *North Carolina Archives and History*. Bottom: Thomas Blount Hill House, Tillery, c. 1793, with its plan. *Frances Benjamin Johnston, Library of Congress*

house at Halifax, which would appear, from a single old photograph, to date from the immediate post-Revolutionary period.

Alas, many of these beautiful Palladian farm houses have been demolished and few of those which survive have been documented. William Bethel, whose father had come from Virginia and settled in a part of Guilford County now in Rockingham County, was a state legislator for fourteen years. He built one of the earliest three-part houses between Lick Fork and Hogan's Creek about 1790. It burned about 1933. Solomon Graves's house at Yanceyville was also built in the 1790's, with the typical T-plan and long hall running across the front of the center block. Bricks are used to fill the spaces between the studs and braces of its timber-framed walls. Although the building still stands with a handsome modillion cornice, it is in a sad state of decay and lacks its original porch and panelled shutters. Thomas Blount Hill's house at Tillery, known as The Hermitage, was built about 1793, with the typical T-plan, two-story central block and one-story wings. With an elaborate modillion cornice, eccentric frontispiece, raked weatherboarding in the pediment and panelled wainscot, Hill's house is an excellent example of late Georgian design. Ayr Mount, a large brick three-part house at Hillsborough, built for William Kirkland sometime before 1810, is almost high style in its grandeur. The Flemish bond walls, bold modillion cornice, moulded sills, watertable, gauged brick and panelled overmantels suggest that Ayr Mount may have been built in the 1790's. Whitmel Hill Pugh House was built near the village of Woodville in 1801. Although the chimneys have been rebuilt, one original brick bears the date "1801." The front-facing gable forms a pediment with a handsome Palladian window and modillion cornice. Inside, the parlor chimneypiece is ornamented with carved ovals and diamonds and reeding. The stair has the turned balusters and flat handrail of the late Georgian period.

The so-called Sally-Billy House, originally located just west of Scotland Neck, was built for Lewis Bond. The date "1808" is scratched in a chimney brick. The interior stair is embellished with Chinese Chippendale latticework. The Sally-Billy House was moved about twenty miles to Halifax in 1974 and, now restored, is open to the public. Shady Oaks, built for Robert Tines Cheek about 1812 near Fishing Creek and Opossum Quarter near Warrenton, has decorated step ends, an unusual sunburst panel under the stair and gougework mantels. Like the undocumented John Harris House, which once stood near Scotland Neck, Shady Oaks has a central block which projects as a true pavilion beyond the walls of the one-story wings. Little is known of what was probably

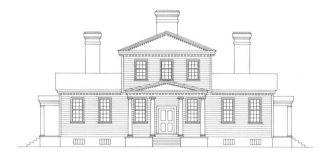

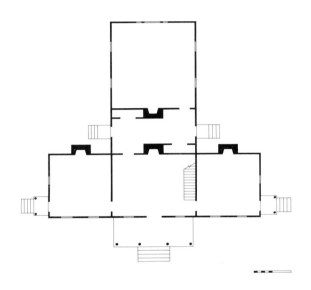

Elevation and plan of The Grove, Halifax, c. 1790.

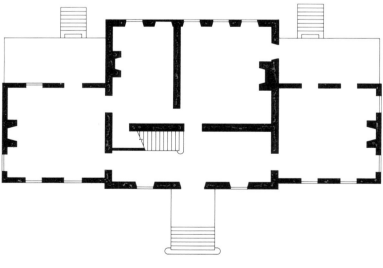

Ayr Mount, William Kirkland House, Hillsborough, c. 1800, with its plan.

Ayr Mount, parlor.

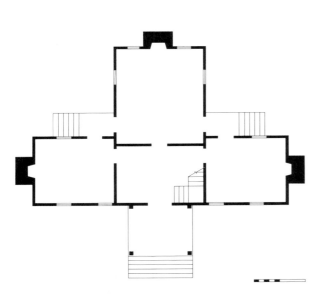

Top: Sally-Billy House, Scotland Neck, 1808, with its plan. *Historic American Buildings Survey, Library of Congress.* Bottom: Shady Oaks, Robert Tines Cheek House, Warrenton vicinity, c. 1812. *Frances Benjamin Johnston, Library of Congress*

Left: Sally-Billy House, stair. Right: Shady Oaks, stair.

Reid-Williams-Macon House, Airlie vicinity, c. 1810, undocumented.
Frances Benjamin Johnston, Library of Congress

one of the last and best of these three-part houses, the so-called Reid-Williams-Macon House, which once stood three miles south of Airlie. This elegant little building had a tall foundation of coursed stone, with modillion cornice, semicircular fanlight entrance and demilune window in its central pediment. It would appear to have been built about 1810, but, because its exact location is unknown, documentation is difficult.

The builders of these three-part farm houses had been inspired, at a distance, by Palladio, the late 16th-century Italian designer who had himself been inspired by ancient Roman architecture. But it was not until the 18th century that the modern world rediscovered the everyday life of the ancient world, and its domestic architecture, revealed by excavations which began at Herculanaeum in 1735 and at Pompeii in 1755. Robert Wood and James Dawkins described Roman antiquities of the Syrian desert in their publications. *The Ruins of Palmyra*, 1753, and *The Ruins of Balbec*, 1757. Such archaeological discoveries, published in sumptuous illustrated folios, became models for a new kind of classical architecture in the last third of the 18th century in England. This neoclassical style took its name from the Scottish architect and designer Robert Adam, who once described himself as "antique-mad." Born at Edinburgh in 1728, Adam was the second son of Scotland's most important architect. In 1758, after four years' study in Italy, Adam, with his brothers James and William, established an architectural office in London. In 1764 he published a book of his own about late Roman ruins located in what is now Yugoslavia, *The Ruins of the Palace of the Emperor Diocletian at Spalatro*.

Instead of the Renaissance's generalized, monumental forms, copied mostly from ancient public buildings, designers could now imitate specific, cozy details of private dwellings. Adam complained that the old Palladian buildings were "ponderous," while real Roman design was "all delicacy, gaiety, grace." In place of Palladianism's cool, impersonal, solemn, splendid grandeur, Adam's neoclassicism was cheerful, personal, vivacious, intimate. Adam's architectural practice—and his style—were concerned primarily with interior decoration. Rooms, which had earlier been almost uniformly rectangular, were now given a variety of shapes to reflect their various uses, with vaults, niches, oval or round ends and columnar screens—all inspired by late Roman planning. Adam filled his rooms with intricate decoration—anthemia, rinceaux, urns, garlands, medallions, paterae—and often highlighted them with bright, light paint colors. Mouldings and cornices were flattened, proportions lengthened. Where Palladian architecture had been monumental, masculine, muscular, this neoclassicism was intimate, feminine, graceful.

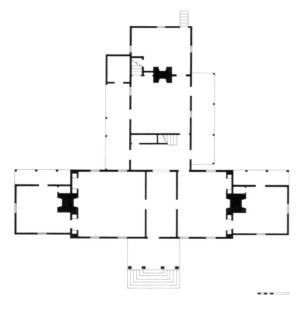

Elevation and plan of Little Manor, William Person Little House, Littleton, c. 1804.

In England, Adam's fame reached its peak in the 1770's, but the style associated with his name did not cross the Atlantic until after the Revolution. He died in 1792, but his influence continued to dominate the American architectural scene for thirty more years. It simply took time for tastemakers to write and publish the books which would spread this new style. William Pain was one of the most successful popularizers of Adam architecture for carpenters and housewrights. *The Practical Builder*, originally published in London in 1774, was not issued in America until 1792; *The Practical House Carpenter* of 1784 was not issued in America until 1796; and his *Carpenter's Pocket Directory* of 1781 did not appear in America until 1797. Asher Benjamin of Massachusetts published the first American architectural handbook in 1797.

Adam's neoclassicism, simplified as it crossed the ocean, became what is now called in America the Federal style. Proportions of buildings, rooms, doors, cornices, mouldings and baseboards became thinner, lighter, more delicate, partly because they were so often copied from engravings in books. Circular motifs were favored—oval or round-ended rooms, round-headed windows set under relieving arches and cascading spiral stairs. Simple tapering spindles and round handrails replaced the heavily turned balusters and flattened handrails of the mid-18th century. Swirling patterns of surface decoration on doors and window frames and mantels were executed in cast plaster or carved wood. Marble mantels were decorated with a frieze of carved classical figures, while wood mantels were embellished with plaster ornaments cast in the form of garlands or carved sunbursts or flat geometric designs. Instead of the heavy panelling associated with mid 18th-century taste, walls were now plastered above a simple chairrail.

Little Manor, now a solitary ruin surrounded by dense woods and barbed wire near the village of Littleton, was one of the great Federal houses of North Carolina. Though Little Manor has a two-story central block with one-story wings, it is not truly typical of the era's three-part, Palladian-inspired houses. In fact, Little Manor is the enlargement, made about 1804 by William Person Little, of an earlier dwelling, built by his uncle Thomas Person, which became the base of its T-shaped plan. Unlike the other three-part houses of North Carolina, Little Manor has a central hall which leads, through an arched doorway, into a transverse stair hall at the rear. Little Manor was also far larger in scale, more opulent in finish and more inventive in decorative detail than any other houses of the period in North Carolina. The first-floor front windows rest on panelled aprons flanked by pilasters and are surmounted by entablatures. The central block, with its modillion cornice and wooden

Little Manor, exterior view. *Frances Benjamin Johnston, Library of Congress*

Little Manor, interior views, this page and opposite.
Frances Benjamin Johnston, Library of Congress

stringcourse, is a true pavilion which projects beyond the front of the wings. The front foundation wall and the tall, tapering chimneys are constructed of crisply carved, tightly fitted stone. With its delicate cornices, cast plaster ornament, arched niches and grand scale, Little Manor was one of North Carolina's few truly sumptuous houses.

In 1800 New Bern was the largest town of North Carolina, with 2567 people—compared with 1689 in Wilmington, 1565 in Fayetteville and 1302 in Edenton—but only one-eighth the size of Charleston in South Carolina. Of New Bern's four hundred buildings, only the colonial Palace, the jail, a church and two houses were built of brick. The port's most important trade was with New England, the source of important newcomers, architectural talent and money. The handsome First Presbyterian Church on New Street looms over the town like a white New England meeting house on a village green. Its cornerstone was laid in June, 1819, by builders Uriah Sandy, John Dewey and Martin Stevenson. The church was dedicated in January, 1822. The interior, remodelled in the late 19th century, was recreated in the 1930's.

The most typical urban dwelling of the early 19th century was a three- or four-story, three-bay building with a side-hall plan. It was a concept so simple and so practical that it was used in port cities all along the eastern coast of America from Boston to Savannah. During the late 18th century, elegant examples of this type were published by Robert and James Adam in their *Works in Architecture* and simpler versions were published by Asher Benjamin in his *American Builder's Companion* of 1806. These textbook models were shown without windows in their side walls, because they were intended to be built beside older buildings or as rows in congested cities like London or Boston. At New Bern, several builders, including Martin Stevenson, John Dewey, Asa King and their assistants, copied this model as a free-standing house and embellished it with exuberant Adamesque woodwork. The typical New Bern house was two and one-half stories, with gable roof, dormers, brick walls laid in Flemish bond, modillion eaves cornice and side-hall plan. Each had a wooden porch with a Palladian-inspired pediment and arched soffit, supported by slender, often paired, colonettes. The gable wall adjacent to the hall typically had an arched window flanked by quadrant windows, suggesting a three-part Diocletian or thermal window. (Popular in the Federal era, it was so called because it was modelled on the ancient Baths, or thermae, of Diocletian.) Below this window, on the ground story, a door led from the hall into a side garden or to an adjacent office. The visitor is most impressed by the delicate interiors, with transverse arches dividing the front hall from the rear stair

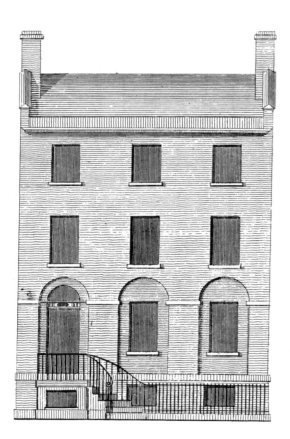

"A Small Town House," from Asher Benjamin's *The American Builder's Companion* (Boston, 1806). *Private Collection*

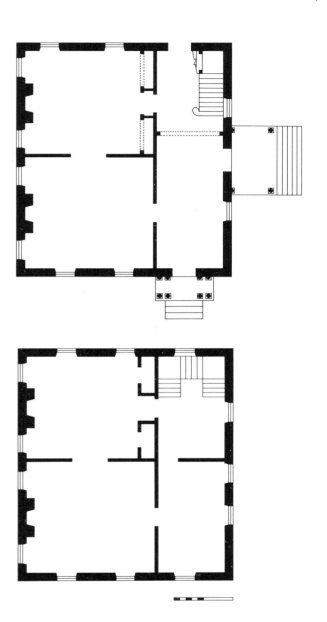

Top: Eli Smallwood House, 524 East Front Street, New Bern, c. 1810. Bottom: John Donnell House, Craven Street, New Bern, 1816–17. *Private Collection*. Right: Plan of first and second stories of Smallwood House.

John Donnell House, interior. *Frances Benjamin Johnston, Library of Congress*

Eli Smallwood House, second-story parlor.

Mulberry Hill, Dr. Frederick S. Blount House, Edenton vicinity, c. 1815, with a view
of its hall, opposite. The original porch has been destroyed. *Frances Benjamin
Johnston, Library of Congress*

hall, pediments and entablatures framing doors and windows and fancy paintwork imitating luxurious woods and marble.

Martin Stevenson was the builder of the house and adjacent office of James Bryan, a lawyer, at 605 Pollock Street in 1802–04. Stevenson was born in 1776 and apprenticed to Joseph Palmer in 1790 at the age of fourteen as a house carpenter and joiner. He also operated a tavern and sold coffins. When Bryan died before his new house was finished, Stevenson made his coffin! The house was remodelled in the Greek Revival style in 1838 for John Heritage Bryan, who also added a dining room. Stevenson died in 1849. John Dewey, who also built and possibly designed the Palladian-inspired Masonic Hall at New Bern, began the house of Frederick Jones at 528 East Front Street about 1810. The house was completed in 1816 for Moses Jarvis of Fairfield, Connecticut. Asa King was the builder of Eli Smallwood's house at 524 East Front Street, about 1810, and of the house of John Donnell, an Irish-born lawyer and judge, on Craven Street, in 1816–17. Donnell's account book records that the stone steps, sills, iron railings, locks and columns for the front porch came from New York.[25] It was destroyed in 1970. Mulberry Hill, outside Edenton, was built about 1815, overlooking Albemarle Sound, for Dr. Frederick S. Blount after his marriage to Rachel Bryan. She was the widow of James Bryan, which explains how a house of the distinctive, urban New Bern type came to be built on a plantation elsewhere in North Carolina.[26]

What the country builder could not execute in plaster or carved wood he might imitate with paint or paper. George Ladner, a painter, gilder and glazier "lately from New-York," was in Edenton in June, 1788, offering "mahogany-graining to its perfection" and "marbeling after the Italian method."[27] John Perkins's house, near the Catawba River outside Newton, was probably begun in the 1790's, a simple, gable-roofed brick structure on a low fieldstone foundation. The interior, however, was ornamented, perhaps about 1810, with panelled wainscot, an elaborate cornice and a complicated chimneypiece which combined panels, pilasters, consoles, urns, foliage and swags in a mixture of late Georgian and frontier Federal design, all of which was grained, marbled and highlighted with bold colors. An upstairs chimney breast was ornamented with a fanciful painting of a tree of life, around the trunk of which a serpent coiled. In 1819 William Williams, artist and art teacher at New Bern, offered to paint cornices "in the best and most elegant manner."[28] Gold and silver leaf, Venetian red, Spanish brown, Prussian blue, Turkey umber, vermillion, patent yellow and Verdigris were among many colors offered for sale at Raleigh between 1804 and 1817. In

Chimneypiece with graining, marbleizing and decorative painting from John Perkins
House, Newton vicinity, c. 1790, interiors completed in early 19th century.
Museum of Early Southern Decorative Arts, Winston-Salem

Graining and marbleizing in second-story hall at William Fewell House,
Madison vicinity, c. 1820.

April, 1819, John Ruse, paperhanger, set up shop at Mr. Ruffin's hotel, Raleigh, where he exhibited for sale French wallpapers, including views of Captain Cook's voyages, published by Dufour at Paris in 1804.[29] William Fewell's house, outside Madison, built about 1820, is now in ruins, but the remarkable decorative paintwork, imitating maple and granite, is still beautiful. Alexander Shaw's house near Wagram was decorated by an itinerant artist named I. or J. Scott in 1836. The parlor from this house, with its "Vue of New-York" above the mantel, grained panelling, marbled baseboards and a frieze of painted tassels and swags, all applied on the flush board walls, is now at the Abby Aldrich Rockefeller Folk Art Center, Williamsburg.

Architectural books showed country builders how to draw plans and elevations, to copy rich decorative details conceived by professional designers, to calculate the complicated geometry of stairs and proper proportions of the classical orders and costs. In November, 1831, and April, 1832, while David Hampton and Jacob Shuman were working on James Torrence's house, Cedar Grove, near Huntersville, they purchased copies of builder's handbooks written by Asher Benjamin and Peter Nicholson. (These transactions are recorded in the ledger of Torrence, who was the local storekeeper as well as owner of Cedar Grove.)[30] Although Asher Benjamin, the Massachusetts housewright who published many builder's handbooks in many editions, was probably the most important architectural writer in early 19th-century America, the single most influential handbook in North Carolina seems to have been Owen Biddle's *Young Carpenter's Assistant*, first published at Philadelphia in 1805, reissued in at least eight editions and still in print in the 1850's. Biddle's design for a stair, with its distinctive step-end, was probably the most often copied design in 19th-century North Carolina. Biddle also illustrated decorative urns, to be carved in relief on mantels and entablatures, another detail favored by North Carolina builders.

Venetian windows, first popularized by early 18th-century English editions of Palladio and favored by the Adam brothers in the 1760's, were illustrated throughout the late Georgian period in the architectural books used by American builders. John Hawks had used a Venetian window in his early, discarded design for the Governor's Palace at New Bern in the late 1760's. In the Federal era, enthusiasm for them was so great that one Venetian window was simply not enough to satisfy an ambitious North Carolina builder. In 1829 Duncan Cameron, deciding to move from his farm outside Durham to Raleigh, asked builder J. H. Smith to prepare drawings for a new house. The house was never built, but Smith's delightful sketch shows a hip-roofed structure with five Palladian windows and a Palladian doorway as well![31]

Plate 31, design for a stair, from Owen Biddle's *Young Carpenter's Assistant* (Philadelphia, 1805), was the model for many North Carolina houses, including Graham House, Lincoln County. *Biddle illustration from North Carolina Collection, University of North Carolina. Photograph by Frances Benjamin Johnston, Library of Congress*

Collins House, Franklin County, undocumented.

William Dortch's house in Nash County, built between 1800 and 1810, is a conventional, two-story, gable-roofed, central-hall frame farm house. But the talented housewright chose to embellish the exterior with a denticulated modillion cornice and many three-part windows, each flanked by fluted Ionic pilasters with moulded bases and fully carved capitals. The first-story windows have round-headed centers with keystones, and the second-story windows bear elaborate entablatures. The best parlor and hall have modillion cornices and urn-shaped saw-work decorations over the doors and windows. The so-called Collins House, yet undocumented, was built in Franklin County, between Louisburg and Centerville. It is another two-story, gable-roofed frame farm house, but the builder added five Palladian windows and a Palladian entrance. In the best rooms, the talented builder inserted blind arches over the doors and side windows to imitate the round-headed Palladian windows of the front wall. The house has been moved to Onslow County. The house of Joseph McCain, High Rock, was built about 1808 in the Williamsburg vicinity of Rockingham County. Its walls are laid in common bond, with stone sills and stuccoed arches forming its five flattened Venetian windows.

Warren and Halifax counties, settled mostly by Virginians in the late 18th century and dominated by large tobacco plantations, became North Carolina's richest counties, where a taste for fine building flourished.[32] Montmorenci, the home of William Williams, one of the area's greatest landowners, with five plantations, six thousand acres and ninety slaves, was built near the hamlet of Shocco Springs in Warren County in 1820. An ingenious builder, perhaps following instructions from his cosmopolitan employer, used traditional building forms and materials —a low fieldstone foundation, gable roof, exterior end chimneys and center-hall plan—but revitalized them with careful workmanship and touches of grandeur. A two-story portico, with four pairs of tall, slender columns, an elaborate entablature, a modillion cornice and frieze of garlands, dominated the front facade. The entrance, with its fanlight and sidelights, was flanked by mock-Palladian windows—simple three-part windows surmounted by fanlike decorations. The interior was enriched with cast plaster ornament, gougework, modillion cornices and graining. But the glory of the interior was a free-standing spiral stair. When the stair was disassembled in 1935, it was evident that an inexperienced builder had been able to fabricate such a complicated design only by trial and error. The stair and other parts of the interior were removed in 1935 and later installed at the Henry Francis du Pont Winterthur Museum. (Photographs of the original stair reveal that the installation is far from accurate.) The remaining shell of Montmorenci was demolished in 1940.

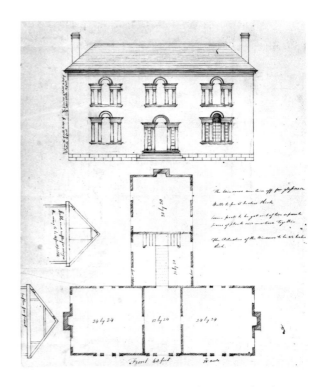

Design for Duncan Cameron's house, Raleigh, drawing by J. H. Smith, 1829. *Cameron Family Papers, Southern Historical Collection, University of North Carolina*

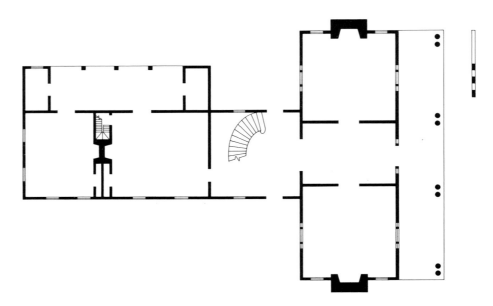

Montmorenci, William Williams House, Warren County, 1820, with its plan.
Henry Francis du Pont Winterthur Museum

Montmorenci, stairhall, before removal. *Winterthur Museum*

Prospect Hill, William Williams Thorne House, Airlie vicinity, c. 1820, with a rear
view and plan, opposite page. *Frances Benjamin Johnston, Library of Congress*

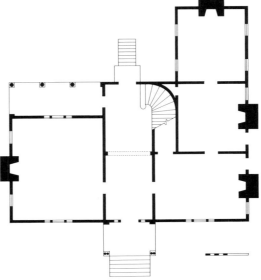

Prospect Hill, chimneypiece. *Frances Benjamin Johnston, Library of Congress*

Top: Prospect Hill, chimneypiece. Bottom: Chimneypiece, Burnside, John Jones House, Williamsboro vicinity, 1818–24. *Frances Benjamin Johnston, Library of Congress*

Burnside, parlor ceiling centerpiece.

William Williams Thorne, a nephew of William Williams, may have employed the same builder to erect his Prospect Hill, in the vicinity of Airlee in Halifax County. This wonderful house has also been demolished. Its portico was supported by pairs of colonettes, the Palladian entrance was flanked by three-part mock-Palladian windows, and the interior stair was decorated with delicate scroll brackets—three distinctive elements found at Montmorenci as well. Burnside, in the Williamsboro vicinity of Vance County, was built for John Jones about 1800 and remodelled by Dr. Thomas Hunt between 1818 and 1824. The exuberant gougework carving and complicated plasterwork garlands, mouldings and acanthus leaves in the parlor recall the work at Montmorenci and Prospect Hill. Dr. Little H. Coleman's house in Warrenton, built 1821–25, has the mock-Palladian windows used at Montmorenci and Prospect Hill and the same ceiling centerpiece used at Burnside. Without further documentation, it is hard to say whether the apparent connection between these fine houses was the result of family association, neighborhood imitation or one talented craftsman and his apprentices.

Another accomplished builder seems to have been responsible for a group of substantial brick houses near Morganton in the 1820's. Two houses are distinguished by the use of Flemish-bond walls, flat arches with gauged brick or segmental relieving arches over window openings, roof eaves formed by brick corbels, and a simple plan with two entrance doors and no central hall. Both had unusual two-tiered porches set under the left rear gable, and both interiors were finished with plaster walls over panelled wainscot, plaster cornices and sunburst mantels. Bellevue, the home of James Irwin, was built between 1823 and 1827. A carpenter named Jonas Bost billed Irwin for flooring, wainscotting, cornices, windows, blinds, doors, staircases, chimneypieces and a piazza in April, 1827. Bost, of Lincoln County, was born in 1794 and died in 1870. Though listed in census reports as a carpenter, he was also a farmer, court officer, director of a plank road and a railroad promoter. He supervised carpentry at William Strickland's Branch Mint in Charlotte in 1836–38. Bellevue is in an excellent state of preservation, although its front porch has been rebuilt and the rear porch has been altered. Pleasant Vailey, built for Alfred Perkins sometime before 1829, burned in 1977. The grandfathers of both Irwin and Perkins were early settlers who had come to the Catawba River Valley in the mid-18th century. A third house, Cedar Grove, built for Jacob Forney in 1825, may have been built by the same hands. It has lost its original interior, except for one tall Georgian mantel, and gained a long Victorian front porch.

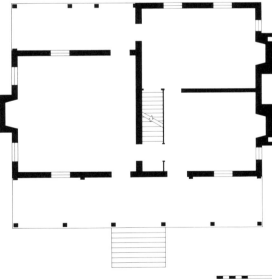

Alfred Perkins House, Morganton vicinity, before 1829, with its plan. *Frances Benjamin Johnston, Library of Congress*

Academy, New Bern, 1806–09, as illustrated on Jonathan Price's 1822 map and seen in photograph of unrestored building. *Map illustration from North Carolina Archives and History. Frances Benjamin Johnston, Library of Congress*

It was to this world of traditional buildings and untaught carpenters and housewrights that William Nichols came from England about 1800.[33] Nichols, born at Bath in 1777, was a professional architect, described by William Tathum in a letter to Albert Gallatin in 1806 as "a Clerk, Draftsman, Surveyor, Architect and regular bred Workman, of considerable talents, ingenuity and merit." Until 1806 Nichols remained at New Bern, whose Academy, which replaced an earlier wooden structure of the 1760's, has been attributed to him, as well as to others. Built in 1806–09, the Academy, with its hipped roof and projecting pavilion, was another Palladian structure much like the State House at Raleigh, Old South at the University, the academy at Wilmington and the Masonic Hall at New Bern. Nichols's design for the Academy's semicircular portico may have been copied from George Richards's *New Vitruvius Britannicus*, published at London in 1802.

Between 1806 and 1818, Nichols worked at Edenton, where he designed a spire for St. Paul's Church. (The spire still stands but without the Adamesque urns that once embellished the corners of its base.) Nichols's most important creation at Edenton was the house at Hayes, a plantation east of the city on land bounded by Queen Anne's Creek, Edenton Bay and Albemarle Sound. It is a two-story frame house with shingled, hipped roof, large louvered cupola and modillion eaves cornice. The principal front has a two-story Doric portico with gallery. Fanlight doorways, with panes stencilled with colorful floral designs and architraves embellished with early use of Greek ornament, lead into a central hall with a steep spiral stair. Quadrant passageways, colonnades of paired Tuscan columns, originally floored with planks, are flanked with storerooms and lead to gabled wings, one of which is a library, the other a stone-paved kitchen.

In 1814, James Johnston, a lawyer who devoted his life to agriculture, was given Hayes by his father, Samuel, who had purchased the plantation in 1765. We know that John Hawks, the famous architect of colonial North Carolina, sent some drawings to Samuel Johnston in 1773. Family tradition has always maintained that Hayes was built between 1789, the year before Hawks died, and 1801, a date inscribed on one of the foundation stones. A map of Hayes, dated December 28, 1812, shows a sketch of a two-story house with colonnades and dependencies like the present house at Hayes but without a hipped roof, cupola or monumental portico. In 1814, James Johnston wrote that Hayes then had "a dwelling house and out-house out of repair and uninhabitable."[34] It is curious that the wings at Hayes were completely separate from the main body of the house—there were no connecting doorways

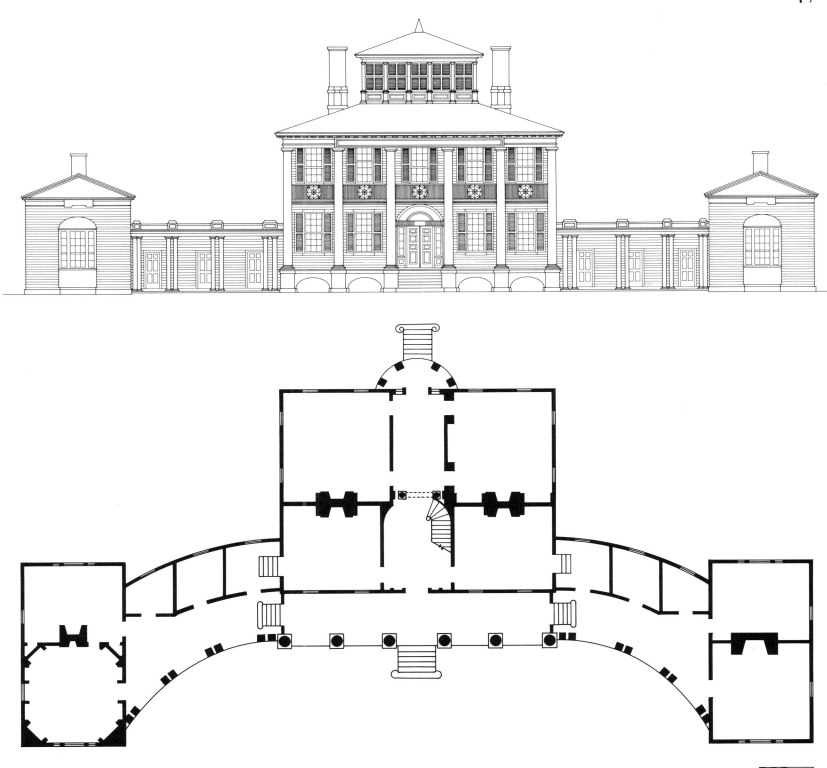

Hayes, James Johnston House, Edenton, before 1817, elevation and plan.

Sketch of an early house at Hayes, detail from an 1812 map. *Hayes Collection, Southern Historical Collection, University of North Carolina*

until recent years—and this suggests that the wings and house, so reminiscent in plan of 18th-century Palladianism, might have been built at different times. Perhaps the present dwelling at Hayes is really an older building, or parts of an older building, substantially rebuilt by William Nichols between 1815 and 1817?

After 1814, when James Johnston received Hayes from his father, the chronology at Hayes becomes clear. In March, 1815, Johnston purchased 100,000 bricks, and in June he purchased feather-edged weatherboarding, planks, rafters, studs, sleepers, tie pins, joists and girders of pine and walnut.[35] By August, materials were ready for building the house and Johnston wrote to a builder in Virginia to come and raise the frame.[36] By the spring of 1817 construction was so far advanced that Johnston sent William Nichols to New York to buy important architectural elements, furniture and decorations for the house. From New York, Nichols wrote to Johnston: "The Steps are in hand, of an excellent Stone, and will be ready in all next week. The railing for Steps and Balcony is undertaken by a very good workman . . . to be finished next week as are also the fanlights. . . . There are only two mantles finished for Sale, of inferior marble and devoid of taste for which they have the impudence to ask $300, so that I have struck that article from the list, being satisfied that with the assistance of composition ornaments I can make any of wood that will answer the purpose much better." Nichols continued with a report on changing taste in early 19th-century America: "Marble or Stone Carving appears to be done away [with] & Cast Iron . . . substituted in all the best houses. Mahogany hand rails are made perfectly round and have a very simple and pleasing effect. I find no difficulty in getting one made from the plan. Their taste in finishing the interior of the Houses in New York is greatly improved, particularly in plaster cornices. How much I regret that we did not get a plasterer from hence. Be pleased, Sir, to inform me if your workmen will undertake plain cornices as I have an opportunity of getting any kind of moulds . . . for cornices are indispensable in the best Rooms & the passage."[37]

In July, 1817, Johnston instructed his friend Joseph Blount, then in New York, to purchase mirrors, two dozen fancy chairs, a settee, a carpet for the drawing room, oil floorcloths for the dining room and hall, fireplace gear, a sideboard, prints (of the Battle of Waterloo, Battle of Bunker Hill, Death of General Montgomery and Trumbull's Declaration of Independence), a complete set of table china, one dozen decanters, wine glasses, silver for two dozen places and other small items, but he added cautiously: "I wish them of the plainest and neatest kind and not in the extreme of fashion but what would suit a moderate liver in

Hayes, exterior view. *Photograph by Bayard Wootten from* Old Homes and Gardens of North Carolina, *with permission of the publisher, The University of North Carolina Press*

State House, Raleigh, as remodelled by William Nichols in the 1820's, detail from a painting by Jacob Marling. *North Carolina Archives and History*

Nancy Mordecai House, Raleigh, portico added by William Nichols, c. 1825. *North Carolina Collection, University of North Carolina*

New York. A man, by appearing very different from his neighbours, is more apt to excite their ridicule and perhaps envy than their esteem and respect. . . . I wish you to have an eye to the latitude & longitude of the place for which they are intended."[38] At the end of October, Johnston, who was unmarried, and his three sisters moved into the completed house at Hayes.[39]

In 1818, William Nichols moved to Fayetteville, the principal market-place for back-country settlers at the fall line of the Cape Fear River and, with a population of some four thousand people, the most prosperous city of that era in North Carolina. There Nichols built two banks, a public waterworks and other projects. He may have been the designer of St. John's Church, 1817–18, probably the earliest Gothic Revival building in the state. Like most of his other work in Fayetteville, the church was destroyed by a calamitous fire in 1831.

In 1819 Nichols was appointed Superintendent of Public Buildings and State Architect of North Carolina. In 1818 he had drawn a new cupola for the old State House and between 1820 and 1824 he continued to supervise its extensive remodelling. His purchases of gin and whiskey for the laborers were dutifully recorded in the official receipts.[40] A third story and gable roof were added, two projecting pavilions were enlarged into temple fronts with Ionic pilasters and rusticated bases, and the exterior of ill-matching brick was finished with stucco. The interior was rearranged, creating a tall domed rotunda at the center to exhibit Antonio Canova's statue of Washington, which reached Raleigh in December, 1821, and embellishing the legislative halls. The interior was described in October, 1821: "The Senate Chamber is in a circular form . . . with a commodious Gallery, supported by twelve Pillars of the Greek Ionic order. The Commons Hall is of semi-elliptical form . . . with a Gallery and Vaulted Ceiling, supported by a Peristyle of Columns." These rooms contained "a large spread eagle made of brass" above each window, "Turkey carpet" on the floors, "an elligant brass candlestick [chandelier]" and curtains of "a clouded blue or purple" color.[41] The remodelled State House burned in 1831.

In the 1820's, Southern builders were experimenting with more monumental designs. Montmorenci and Hayes had their great two-story porticoes. At Old Sparta, a crossroads five miles north of Tarboro, Peter Evans added a two-tiered recessed porch to Piney Prospect, an earlier house built about 1800. Sometime about 1825 William Nichols added new rooms and a two-tiered portico, perhaps the first of its kind in the state, to Nancy Mordecai's house in Raleigh, which had been built in 1785 for Henry Lane. In 1825 Nichols designed and built a brick State

Ingleside, David Forney House, Iron Station, 1817.
Frances Benjamin Johnston, Library of Congress

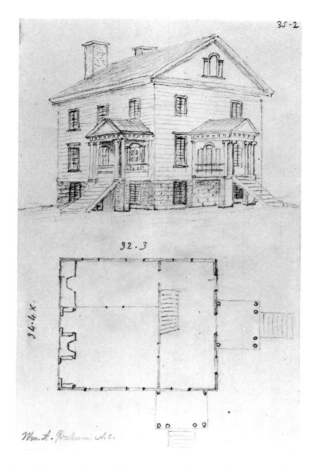

In urban settings, the commanding gable ends of houses were oriented towards gardens, away from the street and clearly subordinated to the front entrances. In rural settings, the importance of "front" and "side" entrances became ambiguous or reversed. Montrose, Hillsborough vicinity, drawing by A. J. Davis. *Avery Library*

Treasurer's office facing Capitol Square. It was demolished in 1840. In 1826 he is believed to have added a monumental Ionic portico to the Governor's House, which had been built in 1814–16. Between 1822 and 1827, Nichols designed and built the Old West building and Gerrard Hall (completed finally in 1837) at the University of North Carolina and added a third story to its Old East building. Nichols also designed the Masonic Lodge at Hillsborough, 1823–25, with a glazed observatory and gallery on its roof, and at least two courthouses. The architect of Ingleside, a two-story brick house built near Iron Station in Lincoln County in 1817 for David Forney, is unknown, but its commanding two-story Ionic portico recalls those at Gerrard Hall and the Governor's House, a design which Nichols seems to have introduced to North Carolina and then continued to employ throughout his career. In 1827 Nichols moved to Alabama, where he became State Architect and later State Engineer. In 1833 he became Assistant State Engineer in Louisiana, and three years later he moved to Mississippi as State Architect. Nichols died at Lexington, Mississippi, in 1853.

In the northern and eastern parts of North Carolina, a new kind of temple-like house was being built in the 1820's.[42] Like the Palladian farm houses of 1790–1810, the gables of these buildings face forward, creating the appearance of a pediment. But these houses were new and different, not an evolution of that older type. The old Palladian farm houses had a single room behind the front hall, stairs which rose steeply or awkwardly and one-story side wings. But the temple-like houses of the 1820's always have two rooms behind the front hall, substantial stairs which ascend to landings, often behind a decorative arch, and, instead of wings, there are side porches. The Palladian farm houses had T-shaped plans derived from 18th-century England. The temple-like houses of the 1820's adapt the side-hall plan of 19th-century America, like those so popular at New Bern. Important side entrances and decorative windows under the side gable had been important features of the fine brick houses at New Bern. By pivoting the plan of these houses ninety degrees, the side hall becomes a lateral front hall, front and rear porches become highly ornamental side porches, and best of all, the side gable with its decorative windows becomes a heroic front for these new temple-like houses. It was a brilliant, though probably serendipitous, adaptation of an urban house for a rural setting.

Mount Petros, near Inez, in Warren County, was built for Dr. Solomon Williams about 1819. It has been demolished. Oakland, at Airlie, was probably built for the niece of William Williams, owner of Montmorenci, and her husband, Henry Hill Thorne, about 1823. Its porch has been reconstructed, and the side porches are no longer standing. Dalkeith, the home of John Burgess, the brother of Melissa Williams of Montmorenci, was built about 1825 near Arcola. The Morgan House, in the vicinity of South Mills, was built about 1826. The pediment bears a large lunette window, and the porch has an arched soffit with keystone. Elgin, outside Warrenton, was built between 1827 and 1832 for Peter Mitchel. The pediment is embellished with a modillion cornice and striking Doric entablature. At Louisburg, William P. Williams added a temple-like addition to a late 18th-century house sometime after he purchased it in 1822.[43] Similarly, John A. Williams added a two-room temple front to an earlier house, Shady Grove, near Inez, about 1830.

North Carolina builders, trained by apprenticeship and experience, were slow to adopt new styles. When the Market Hall at Fayetteville, built in 1788, burned in 1831, the authorities decided to rebuild it with an octagonal belfry, Ionic pilasters, roof balustrade and open loggia—an English Georgian town hall in 19th-century North Carolina! Anna Maria Ward's house at Mount Olive, sometimes known as Vernon or the Hatch-Kornegay House, was built about 1837, a two-story frame house with wide double doors and an immense semicircular fanlight. The interior was decorated with an eccentric mélange of Georgian-Federal ornament, including broken pediments, sunbursts, heavy engaged columns, trefoil and foliated sawwork. In the following year, the builder of Dongola, Jeremiah Graves's house at Yanceyville, added a massive Doric entablature and two-story portico to an otherwise conventional late Federal house. Eaton Place, built about 1842 at Warrenton, also combines Federal and Greek Revival details, including a fanlight which impinges on a Doric entablature. Country builders preferred to repeat the traditional, though old-fashioned, designs they knew so well.

Oakland, Henry Hill Thorne House, Airlie, c. 1823.

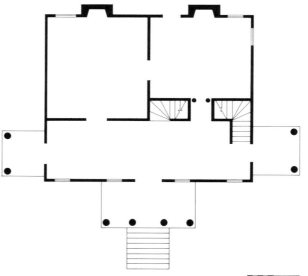

Dalkeith, John Burgess House, Arcola vicinity, c. 1825, with its plan.

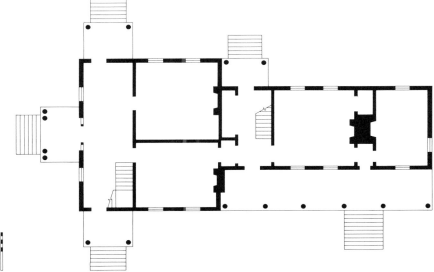

Elgin, Peter Mitchel House, Warrenton vicinity, 1827–32, a 19th-century
photograph and plan. *Private Collection*

Elgin, exterior view and, opposite page, interior.

Morgan House, South Mills vicinity, c. 1826.

Anna Maria Ward House, Mount Olive, c. 1837, interior view.
Frances Benjamin Johnston, Library of Congress

IV. *The Greek Revival*

The Greek Revival, which became the most widespread and most genuinely popular architectural style of 19th-century America, has been explained as an expression of the nation's youthful democratic ideals, inspired by the War of 1812 and inflamed by the Greek rebellion against the Turks in the 1820's. But the Greek Revival is better understood as part of a great artistic movement which began to sweep across the Western world at the end of the previous century. James Stuart and Nicholas Revett had begun publication of their *Antiquities of Athens* in 1762. The ancient monuments illustrated in these volumes—especially the Choragic Monument of Lysicrates, the Temple of Ilissus and the Tower of the Winds—became part of the 19th century's architectural vocabulary. A. J. Davis, the New York architect who was one of the designers of the North Carolina Capitol at Raleigh, purchased a copy of Stuart and Revett's book from his partner Ithiel Town in May, 1831, and dated the start of his professional career from the day he first saw those volumes at the Boston Athenaeum.[1]

Greek details had first appeared in American books with John Haviland's *The Builder's Assistant*, published at Philadelphia in 1818. The more old-fashioned Massachusetts housewright Asher Benjamin did not include Greek details in his books until the sixth edition of *The American Builder's Companion* in 1827. But three years later, in his *Practical House Carpenter*, Benjamin observed: "Since my last publication, the Roman School of architecture has been entirely changed for the Grecian." Except for the monumental Greek portico at Hayes, by an English architect ahead of taste in America, the earliest use of the Greek Revival in North Carolina was probably a handsome porch which Duncan Cameron added to Fairntosh, north of Durham, in 1827, when his sister wrote: "The carpenters are building a piazza in front of the house." Cameron had come to North Carolina from Virginia in the 1790's and built his large, two-story frame house at Fairntosh in 1810. Cameron soon demonstrated so much ambition, ability and determination as a

Fairntosh, Duncan Cameron House, Durham vicinity, Greek Revival porch added in 1827 to a house built in 1810. *Frances Benjamin Johnston, Library of Congress*

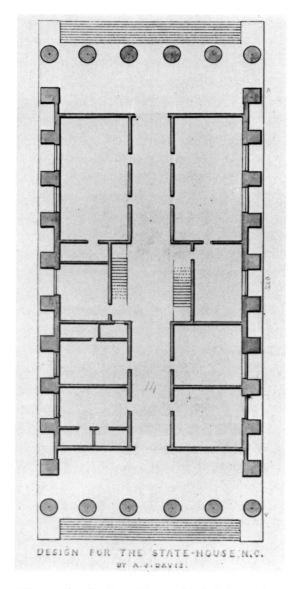

DESIGN FOR THE STATE-HOUSE N.C.
BY A. J. DAVIS.

"Design for the State-House, N.C.," drawn by A. J. Davis, c. 1832. *Avery Library*

planter, lawyer, state legislator and judge that his neighbors prophesied that he would become "as rich as a Jew." As usual Cameron—who at one time employed a seventy-eight-year-old Neopolitan music teacher named Antonio di Martino—was intellectually ahead of his time.[2]

Ironically, the destruction of the first State House, a revered shrine built in the 1790's, was caused by an effort to preserve it.[3] In June, 1831, a workman who was soldering a new fireproof metal roof started a fire which destroyed the old building. The commissioners in charge of building a new Captiol were determined to create another great monument for the state, and it took them ten years, an amount of money equal to three times the state government's annual income and the talents of six architects to complete the work. During construction of the Capitol, these architects sought to build "in strict conformity with Grecian rules,"[4] which meant that details for the Capitol's dome were copied from the Choragic Monument of Lysicrates, the first-floor vestibules from the Ionic Temple of Ilissus, the second-floor lobbies from the octagonal Tower of Andronicus Cyrhestes, and the Senate Hall and rotunda from three different temples on the Acropolis.[5] Significantly, materials and craftsmen from Philadelphia, the first city in America which had embraced the Greek Revival in the 1820's, were vital to the creation of the North Carolina Capitol in the 1830's.

In November, 1831, four months after the fire, Ithiel Town came from New York to Raleigh with a plan and perspective view of his own proposal for a new North Carolina Capitol. Though he had been born in Connecticut and raised in Massachusetts and had practiced architecture in New York, Town had strong North Carolina connections. He had built imposing toll bridges across the Yadkin River at Salisbury and the Cape Fear River at Fayetteville, utilizing his own method of wooden truss construction. Town had already devised a Greek Revival capitol for Connecticut, a temple modelled on the Parthenon, and another for Indiana, a larger temple-like building with a dome. Now Town's office produced another design modelled on the Parthenon for North Carolina. Town's partner, A. J. Davis, worked on plans for the North Carolina Capitol in December, 1832, and two of his preliminary studies survive among his papers.[6] (It is interesting to note that John Stirewalt of North Carolina was working in Town and Davis's office as a "pupil in architecture" for seven months in 1831–32.)[7] In February, 1833, Town sent a perspective sketch "with finished plans" to the commissioners at Raleigh.[8] In the same month, William Gaston, who had served as Town's lawyer in North Carolina, wrote to his daughter and son-in-law, Susan and Robert Donaldson: "The commissioners for rebuilding the State

Capitol have before them Mr. Town's several plans and are well disposed, I think, to adopt whichever Mr. T. shall recommend. I saw several but am so little versed in architecture as not to know which should be preferred. I presume, however, that both Mr. D. and Mr. T. are in favor of that which is without dome, surrounded by columns, and understood to be upon the exact model of the Parthenon."[9]

In January, February and March, 1833, the commissioners met but failed to select a final plan.[10] Meanwhile, the ruins of the old building were being cleared away and stonecutters were starting to prepare material. Despite his persistent efforts and some encouragement, Town's plans were not accepted, when the legislature, after months of debate, decided to make the new Capitol as much like the old State House as possible, "the same as the former building with such extension of length and height as may be deemed necessary." In April, the commissioners adopted the general plan provided by William Nichols, based on his improvements to the old State House made in the 1820's before he moved to Alabama, and hired his son, William Nichols, Jr., who had followed his father in the building trade, to make the final working drawings. Young Nichols delivered his plans to the commissioners in May, 1833, and promised to return to Raleigh whenever architectural advice was needed.[11]

The commissioners were proceeding to manage construction of the Capitol like the building committee of a parish church or village courthouse. Having settled on a plan, they now advertised for workers.[12] They hired William S. Drummond, a builder from Washington who had come to Fayetteville in 1831 to rebuild St. John's Church, as their general superintendent and William Birth, another Washington craftsman, as supervisor of stonecutting and masonry.[13] An experimental railroad was built to transport granite from a state-owned quarry to the construction site. Two primitive cars were pulled over 1.2 miles of track by horses. By May, the ruins of the old building had been removed and foundations for a new structure were begun. By July, the granite walls were three feet high.

But the commissioners soon realized that they had begun the largest building ever attempted in the state and that full-time, experienced professional supervision would be essential. In July, the commissioners turned at last to Ithiel Town. Though the shape and size of the building had already been determined, Town added porticoes to the east and west fronts and all of the specifically Greek details of the exterior. He prepared models to show the commissioners.[14] (The Nichols design was probably Palladian rather than Greek.) In August, Drummond was dis-

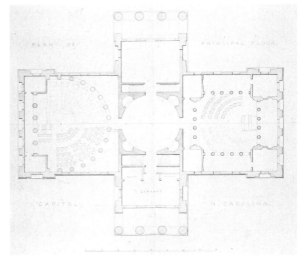

Perspective view and plan of principal story of Town and Davis's North Carolina Capitol, c. 1833. *Metropolitan Museum of Art, Harris Brisbane Dick Fund, 24.66.1401(23) and 24.66.1771*

missed, Birth resigned, and Thomas Bragg, a builder from Warrenton, was put temporarily in charge of day-to-day construction.[15]

In September, 1834, Town hired David Paton, a Scottish architect, to supervise the stone and brickwork.[16] Paton, who described himself as "regularly bred to the profession of Architect and Builder," was born at Edinburgh in 1801, the son and grandson of masons and builders. (His father had subscribed to the final volume of Stuart and Revett's *Antiquities of Athens*.) Paton had worked in Edinburgh during the mid-1820's and had been employed by Sir John Soane in London in 1829–30. (The upstairs passageways at the Capitol, probably designed by Paton, with their springing vaults, thin, flat surfaces and finely chiselled decoration, recall Soane's work.) After the death of his first wife, Paton came to New York in July, 1833. Of Paton, the North Carolina commissioners later wrote: "One thing we are certain of, that he is in his deportment unassuming and gentlemanly—of steady habits and great business talents."[17] By the end of 1834 the southern walls of the Capitol had risen to about forty feet.

New building commissioners were appointed in January, 1835, and they had never met Ithiel Town, far away in New York. In March, without consulting Town, Paton changed the design for the roofs of the legislative chambers. Town had probably devised one of his famous wooden trusses, a design he could be expected to defend with passion equal to his pride, and so he wrote vehemently to Paton: "I am much surprised to find such a free use of your architectural talent in my absence. . . . You were using your utmost powers to impair the confidence of the Commissioners in me & place it in your self as the Architect. . . . Certainly you do not, I presume, intend to place your experience in the science & practice of building on a par with mine! . . . Sooner than be preyed upon in this manner . . . I would furnish the Commissioners with another Superintendent . . . and then do all the Architectural Business for the building—make all working drawings &c. to a complete finish & go there twice or thrice a year & charge *nothing*, not even a *dollar*, for the whole of it!"[18] Meanwhile, in May, 1835, the partnership between Town and A. J. Davis was ended, though Davis continued to do some drawing for his former associate. By the summer, Paton had been appointed "Architect and Superintendent" of the Capitol.

As construction proceeded, problems had to be solved and details had to be filled in, and Paton made further changes and additions to Town's designs, just as Town had revised those of his predecessor. Majestic stairs, intended as grand entrances to the central rotunda, were simplified and moved into lobby passageways. The Supreme Court and State

North Carolina Capitol, Raleigh, 1833–40.

North Carolina Capitol, second-story passage.

Library were moved to the third floor, making space for offices and committee rooms on the lower stories. Paton prepared drawings for galleries in the legislative halls, plus other innumerable details. In 1836, Robert Mills advised Paton on the use of copper and zinc to cover roofs, recommending zinc, because it was cheaper.[19] Between 1836 and 1840, to be sure his designs were in "strict observance of the rules of Architectural taste," Paton submitted some of his drawings to William Strickland of Philadelphia for approval.[20] When Paton left North Carolina in 1840, he carried with him 229 drawings which he had made for the Capitol. (They were destroyed by a descendant who decided to have a house-cleaning bonfire in her backyard about seventy-five years ago.)

The building of the Capitol was, as the commissioners had learned, a tremendous effort.[21] Stones which weighed up to ten tons were cut and finished by hand, hauled to the site by horses and raised into place with ropes, pulleys and muscle power. At times there were some twenty-five carpenters, seventy-five stonecutters and 125 laborers working at the Capitol. The square was littered with heaps of granite, piles of copper for the roof, glass for windows, wooden frames for the roof and the dome ready to be raised into place.[22] In the bitterly cold winter of 1836, as the intricate carving of the porticoes and entablatures was beginning, work had to be suspended for a month. In the spring, the stonecutters began to quit and Paton was dispatched to Philadelphia and New York to recruit new workers. By May, 1837, the exterior of the building was complete except for the western portico and dome.[23] In March, 1838, the workmen were progressing with the interior, building groin arches to support the principal floor and moulding and carving plaster and wooden decorations. Capitals for the House and Senate halls were carved by Joseph Chatterson of Philadelphia. The honeysuckle ornament for the cupola, studs for the doors and stair rails for the rotunda were cast by Wheeler and Cooper of Philadelphia. Copper for the roof, the weights, locks and other hardware all came from Philadelphia. Sixteen chandeliers were provided by the Cornelius family of Philadelphia. Marble mantels were supplied by John Struthers of Philadelphia.

By February, 1840, the first story was complete except for two small rooms and the vestibules. Most of the men were at work on the second story, completing the facings, floors, and windows, installing chimney-pieces in the Hall of Representatives and plastering the Senate Chamber. On the third story the men were fitting doors to the galleries, finishing the stairs to the roof and mounting chimneypieces in the Supreme Court.[24] In May, 1840, though the Court and Library as well as two rooms on the first story were unfinished and no carpets or curtains had

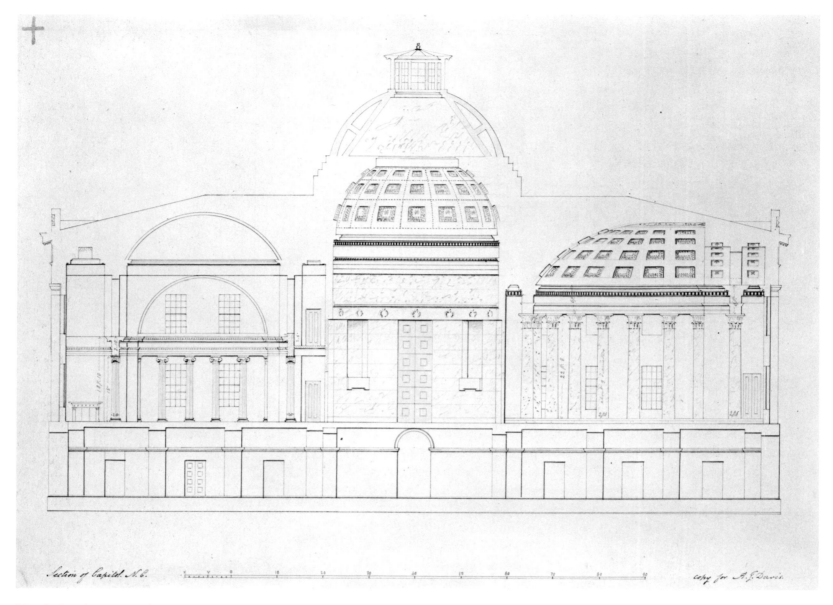

Section of Capitol. N.C.

copy for A. J. Davis

North Carolina Capitol, section, drawn by A. J. Davis, c. 1833. *Metropolitan Museum of Art, Harris Brisbane Dick Fund, 22.66.759*

North Carolina Capitol, rotunda.

North Carolina Capitol, Senate Hall.

North Carolina Capitol, Representatives Hall.

North Carolina Capitol, third-story passageway.

been installed, the impatient commissioners declared the Capitol complete and abruptly dismissed Paton. A celebratory dance was held in the Senate chamber in June, 1840.[25]

The Capitol is a three-story, hip-roofed building, of stone and brick, with a symmetrical cruciform plan and central rotunda, covered with a copper-sheathed dome crowned by cast-iron anthemia. This general plan had been devised by the William Nicholses, modelled on the old State House. Town and Davis discarded the Palladian exterior which the Nicholses had planned and added all its Greek details—the prostyle, pedimented porticoes, which rest on rusticated piers at projections of the east and west walls, the pilasters and Doric entablature, with triglyphs, mutules and guttae. The arrangement of the interior represented the Nicholses' general plan, detailed by Town and Davis and finally rearranged slightly by Paton. The ground story held offices for various government departments. On the second or principal story, a central rotunda led to legislative halls, committee rooms and stairs. In the east and west projections behind the porticoes on the third story were the Supreme Court and State Library, and there were also galleries for the legislative halls. The Capitol was heated by twenty-eight fireplaces. Fortunately, several schemes to enlarge the building were never implemented, and the building has been restored with consummate skill.

In May, 1840, promising to send detailed drawings for completion of the Court Library, Paton left North Carolina and travelled to New York, where A. J. Davis invited him to visit his office. The only other building that Paton is known to have designed in North Carolina was a three-story brick building for the Caldwell Institute, a school at Greensboro, in 1835.[26] In October, 1840, Paton sailed to Scotland, but nine years later he returned to America. Settling in Brooklyn, where he lived until his death in 1882, Paton taught architecture and drawing, while repeatedly, and fruitlessly, petitioning the State of North Carolina for additional compensation for his work on the Capitol.

By the end of the 1830's, Wilmington, on the lower Cape Fear River, had become North Carolina's most important port. In the 1840's, eighteen vessels regularly sailed from Wilmington to New York, nine vessels to Philadelphia, four packets to Boston and four coasters to Charleston.[27] John Norris came to Wilmington from New York in 1839 to supervise construction of Thomas U. Walter's St. James Episcopal Church. Born at New York in 1804, Norris was making the typical progress from mason to builder to architect, as he finally listed himself in the 1847 New York city directory. As supervising architect of St. James, Norris was responsible for hiring laborers, overseeing the work and

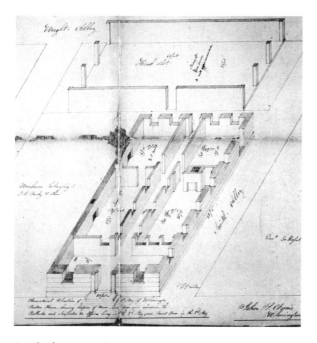

Study for United States Custom House, Wilmington, drawn by John S. Norris, 1843. *National Archives*

purchasing materials and supplies. He remained in North Carolina, off and on, between 1839 and 1846.

Prolonged construction of the Wilmington Custom House took place between May, 1843, and April, 1847, on North Water Street. Robert Mills, the South Carolina-born architect then working in Washington, applied to the Secretary of the Treasury in March, 1843, but John Norris was selected as architect of the Custom House and completed his drawings in July. By February, 1844, the walls had been raised to the second story. But construction lagged, and a year later Murphy Jones, Collector of the Port, complained that Norris was absent from North Carolina for months at a time and, even when he was in Wilmington, often busy elsewhere planning and supervising buildings for private clients. By August, 1845, the second floor had been completed and occupied and the first-story offices were nearly completed, but the vestibule was still unpaved, a mess of loose sand and lime. In May, 1847, the Custom House was finally declared complete. Then in November, 1848, Robert Wood, the local builder whose brother John had applied unsuccessfully for the job of building superintendent, complained to the Treasury Department that the Custom House had been poorly designed and built, with settling foundations, cracking stone walls and water-stained plaster.[28]

The Custom House was a narrow, three-story brick structure, whose gable faced forward to form the pediment of a temple-like front. A rusticated ground story served as a base for two-story engaged, fluted columns, with corner pilasters and cast-iron balcony. The design of the building was described in August, 1845: "The Custom House is three stories high, with attic in rear; has thirty-nine feet front and is sixty-five in depth. It has a pediment front, erected on a basement story of red sand-stone, rusticated. The front has antaes, and two columns, with capitals, after the manner of the Temple of the Winds at Athens, and cornices which is continued on the two sides and returned on the rear, with antaes on rear corners; all being of red sand-stone from Connecticut River. The front, rear and the two flank walls are faced with the celebrated Baltimore pressed brick."[29] The first and second stories contained offices for the post office and customs department. The third story had a domed court and jury room. Doors and window shutters were wrought iron, and the roof was copper plated with iron. The Custom House was destroyed in 1915. After designing a new Greek Revival custom house for Savannah, Norris went to Georgia, where he remained most of the time between 1847 and 1860 and became the most important architect of that place and era. Norris died in 1876.

United States Custom House, Wilmington, 1843–47. *North Carolina Archives and History*

Bank, Washington, 1854, with its possible inspiration, the Temple of Ilissus, as illustrated in Stuart and Revett's *Antiquities of Athens* (London, 1762). *Photograph by Frances Benjamin Johnston, Library of Congress. Book illustration from Avery Library*

In 1838 James Fenimore Cooper satirized the whims of fashion: "The public sentiment just now runs almost exclusively and popularly into the Greecian school. We build little besides temples for our churches and banks, our taverns, our courthouses and our dwellings. A friend . . . has just built a brewery on the model of the Temple of the Winds!" During the first half of the 19th century, as the nation swept across the continent, new state capitols, courthouses, city halls, churches, hospitals and hotels were most likely to be built in the new Greek Revival style. In September, 1844, the Orange County Courthouse, at 106 East King Street in Hillsborough, was begun,[30] designed by the prominent local builder John Berry, who included in his plans a prostyle Doric portico, Doric entablature with triglyphs, metopes and mutules, and an octagonal clock tower and dome. In May, 1854, the directors of the Bank of Washington advertised for someone to build a new banking hall "twenty-five feet front by fifty feet deep, and of proportionable height, the front gable to extend so as to form a Portico supported by four columns, walls of Brick, stuccoed to resemble stone."[31] Their design seems to have been inspired by the famous Ionic Temple of Ilissus, illustrated as Plate III of Stuart and Revett's *Antiquities of Athens*. The Rowan County Courthouse at 200 North Main Street in Salisbury, an important trading town on the principal road headed to the Southwest, was built in 1855, with a monumental Doric portico and entablature and a second-story gallery with cast-iron railing.

The Main Hall of Salem Academy was built in 1855 by Francis Fries. Though A. J. Davis supplied a plan for the Hall, it is unclear if his plan was ever used. A surviving drawing of the Hall, without its heroic Doric portico, was not drawn by Davis. Fries (1812–63), the energetic and talented operator of a woolen factory and paper mill and a state legislator as well, may have designed the Main Hall.[32] The Northampton County Courthouse at Jackson was designed by Henry King Burgwyn and built in 1858–59. The steps and entrance were altered in the late 1930's but the monumental Ionic portico is unchanged. The main building at Chowan Female Institute, now Chowan College, at Murfreesboro, was built in 1851–52 by a builder from Warren County named Albert G. Jones, with a portico 106 feet long! Concord Female College, now Mitchell College, at Statesville, was designed by Jacob Graves of Columbia, South Carolina, and built 1854–56.

In 1850 A. J. Downing, advocate of Romantic design, ridiculed what he called America's "Greek Revival disease." Every house in the country, he wrote, must be a Grecian temple: "Whether twenty feet or two hundred feet front, it must have its columns and portico. There might be

Courthouse, Hillsborough, 1844–45. *Frances Benjamin Johnston, Library of Congress*

Courthouse, 200 North Main Street, Salisbury, 1855. *Frances Benjamin Johnston, Library of Congress*

Academy, Salem, 1855, as seen in early photograph. *Old Salem*

Land's End, James Leigh House, New Hope Township, c. 1830–37.
Frances Benjamin Johnston, Library of Congress

comfortable rooms behind them or not . . . but of what consequence was that if the portico were copied from the Temple of Theseus or the columns were miniature imitations in wood of those of Jupiter Olympus? . . . We build a miserable shed, make one of its ends a portico with Ionic columns and call it a temple in the Greek style!"[33] At its worst, this was what Anthony Trollope in 1861 called the "vilest of architectural pretenses . . . a log of wood called a column . . . vicious bits of timber painted white . . . fixed promiscuously to houses which, without such ornamentation, would be simple, unpretentious, square!"[34]

Of the Greek orders, the Doric was the easiest and cheapest to build, and probably for this reason the most influential books which spread the Greek Revival in North Carolina were Asher Benjamin's *Practical House Carpenter*, 1830, and his *Practice of Architecture*, 1833, both of which featured simple, strong Doric designs.[35] Land's End, in the vicinity of New Hope Township near Albemarle Sound, was built sometime between 1830 and 1837 for James Leigh, a planter and state legislator who was also a skilled carpenter. Its rear door case, mantels and porch entablature are taken from *The Practical House Carpenter*. Creekside, built on a hill near Morganton for George Walton between 1834 and 1837, has mantels copied from plates 50 and 51 of that same work. Ashland, in the Henderson vicinity of Vance County, was remodelled for a second time about 1840, when a new portico and mantel, copied from plate 50, were added. Dr. Shubal Coffin's house on Main Street in Jamestown was also enlarged about 1840 with portico and decorative window frames copied from Asher Benjamin. At Bracebridge Hall, on the Old Sparta Road near the Tar River outside Tarboro, Jonas Carr made Greek Revival improvements to a house which his father had built in 1826.[36] The handsome Doric portico was copied from plate 6 of *The Practical House Carpenter*, the front door case from plate 28, and a chimneypiece was a simplified version of plate 51. The entrance to Philanthropic Hall at Davidson College, dedicated in February, 1850, was copied from plate 28 of Benjamin's *Practice of Architecture*. Elsewhere in America, *The Modern Builder's Guide*, 1833, and *The Beauties of Modern Architecture*, 1835, by New York's Minard Lafever were also popular. But Lafever's designs were more elaborate and so less used in North Carolina. At Pembroke Hall, Matthew Pope's house of the late 1840's on West King Street in Edenton, the columns of the hall were copied from plate 11 of *The Beauties of Modern Architecture*.

All too often these Greek Revival details were merely added to otherwise traditional buildings. But with a bit of courage, the country carpenter could create a more convincing temple-like house by placing a col-

Chimneypiece at Ashland, Henderson vicinity, c. 1840, with its model, Plate 50 of Asher Benjamin's *Practical House Carpenter* (Boston, 1830). *Private Collection*

Ashland, Henderson vicinity, 18th-century house remodelled 1815 and c. 1840.

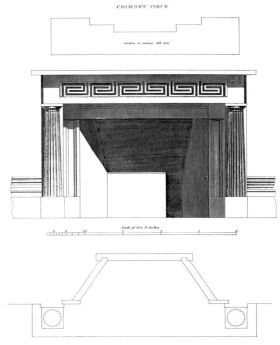

Creekside, George Walton House, Morganton, 1834–37, the parlor with the model
for its chimneypiece, Plate 51 of Benjamin's *Practical House Carpenter*.
Private Collection

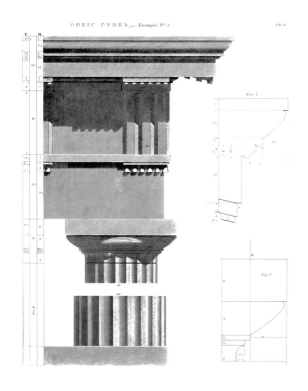

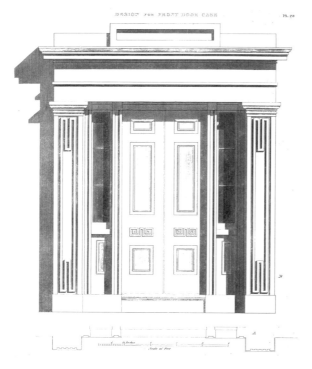

Bracebridge Hall, Jonas Carr House, Tarboro vicinity, early 19th-century house remodelled in 1840's, with the models for its portico and door case, Plates 6 and 28 of Benjamin's *Practical House Carpenter*. *Private Collection*

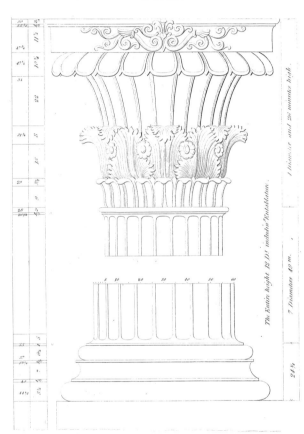

Capital in hall at Pembroke Hall, Matthew Pope House, West King Street, Edenton, late 1840's, with its model, Plate 11 of Minard Lafever's *Beauties of Modern Architecture. Private Collection*

Top: Orton, Wilmington vicinity, as remodelled about 1840, 19th-century view
before early 20th-century additions. Bottom: Will's Forest, Raleigh, 1840–42.
North Carolina Archives and History

umned portico on the short side of a house and running its pediment from a low-pitched gable roof. In 1826 Dr. Frederick J. Hill purchased Orton, a rice plantation on the west bank of the lower Cape Fear River outside Wilmington. The original one-and-one-half story brick house had been built in the second quarter of the 18th century by Roger Moore, the son of an early South Carolina governor who had settled the place in the 1720's. About 1840, Dr. Hill enlarged this old house by adding rear rooms, a transverse stair hall, a second story and Greek Doric portico, whose pediment runs from the gable roof. Will's Forest, Raleigh, was built for Ann Mordecai by Thomas Waitt and Dabney Cosby in 1840–42, with a monumental Ionic portico running from its gable. The house was demolished in 1900. Stockton, built for Josiah

Stockton, Hertford vicinity, late 1840's, with its probable inspiration, frontispiece of Lafever's *Modern Builder's Guide* (New York, 1833). *Photograph by Bayard Wootten, North Carolina Collection, University of North Carolina. Lafever illustration from private collection.*

Granbery outside the village of Hertford in the late 1840's, seems to have been inspired by Lafever's "Design for a Country Villa" in *The Modern Builder's Guide* of 1833. One-story wings flank a two-story central block with a pedimented portico running from its gable roof. Despite the South's popular association with the Greek Revival, there are many more houses modelled on this design in Connecticut, New York, Ohio and Michigan than in the states of the Old South. Stockton is the only example in North Carolina, and none is known in South Carolina or Georgia.

Stockton, Hertford vicinity, late 1840's. *Photograph by Bayard Wootten, North Carolina Collection, University of North Carolina*

As their experience caught up with the evolution of taste, North Carolina builders dared to make their buildings squarer and details heavier. Clover Hill, home of Edmund W. Jones, was built near Patterson in 1846, a two-story, hip-roofed brick building with a one-story Ionic prostyle portico. Trabeated entrances on the first and second stories, with distinctive engaged Ionic columns and pilasters, are used in place of the elliptical fanlights so characteristic of the Federal era. The John A. Taylor House, 409 Market Street, Wilmington, was built in the following year. Taylor operated a ferry across the Cape Fear River, owned a steamship and invested in railroads. Though the designer of Taylor's house is unknown, its bold, audacious severity proclaims the work of a professional architect. Benjamin Gardner, a local builder who designed a Gothic jail for Savannah, Georgia, in 1845, has been associated with it, but John Norris, at the time finishing work on the Custom House in Wilmington, might have been responsible. Of brick construction, with marble veneer, Taylor's house has a recessed central bay, flat roof and cupola. The original interiors have been destroyed except for ceilings, some mantels and cast plaster ornament in the first-story parlors.

The Charles Slover House at 201 Johnson Street in New Bern, built in 1848, has the boxy profile and massive ornament typical of the Greek Revival, with sandstone sills, steps and watertable. During this era, rooms were generally larger and squarer, with plain plaster walls, heavy cornices and tall baseboards and some specifically Greek ornament. The most interesting surviving Greek Revival domestic interior in North Carolina is found at Nathaniel Green's house on West Main Street in Warrenton, built about 1855, probably by the local builder Jacob Holt, with delightful use of Greek meander around doors, windows and stair. Edward Belo, a cabinetmaker turned merchant and industrialist, created an imaginative house at 445 South Main Street in Salem between 1848 and 1859. In 1848 he finished a two-story frame structure, flanked by three-story brick wings. Ten years later he added a third story and Corinthian portico to the center section, as well as cast-iron balcony railings, fences and ornamental statuary from his own foundry. Belo's store operated on the first story, entered through wide doors on Main Street; his residence occupied the second story, entered from a separate portico at another side of the building; his clerks worked on the third story.

John A. Taylor House, 409 Market Street, Wilmington, 1847.

Left: Nathaniel Green House, West Main Street, Warrenton, c. 1855, interior detail.
Right: Marbleizing in hall at Archibald Taylor House, Warren County, c. 1855.
Taylor photograph from North Carolina Archives and History

Charles Slover House, 201 Johnson Street, New Bern, 1848.

Edward Belo House, 445 South Main Street, Salem, 1848–59.
Frances Benjamin Johnston, Library of Congress

V. *Romantic Styles*

In the early 19th century, new engineers, architects and builders came to North Carolina to improve the transportation and trade of the state.[1] Separate companies had been chartered to improve the navigation of the state's principal rivers.[2] In 1816, "a skillful engineer" named James Abernathy, was hired to remove obstructions from the Cape Fear River and build locks and canals.[3] In 1818, David Houston, an engineer from Massachusetts, began to supervise fifty workmen, including masons, blacksmiths and carpenters, whom he had hired in Philadelphia and New York, building locks and canals around the Great Falls of the Roanoke River.[4] Benjamin F. Baldwin, also from Massachuetts, surveyed the Tar and Neuse rivers. In 1819 the legislature hired Hamilton Fulton, an English engineer who had worked in Bermuda, Malta and Sweden, as the official State Engineer. With instruments and supplies purchased in London and an assistant surveyor, Robert H. Brazier, who came with him from England, Fulton surveyed the rivers and harbors and proposed a comprehensive plan for jetties, roads, canals and aqueducts. He supervised construction of a mechanical dredge, which he dubbed "the Bear," whose nine rows of jaw-like iron shovels were supposed to stir up the river bottoms so the ebbing current would carry sand out to sea.[5] So many new artisans had come to North Carolina that, after the calamitous fire of 1831 at Fayetteville, some three hundred workmen were available to come to help rebuild that devastated city.[6] In May, 1837, there were nine hundred laborers at work on the Wilmington and Raleigh Railroad, which opened in 1840.[7]

In the early 19th century, a single housewright—an itinerant artisan or village craftsman—would have worked beside two or three white apprentices and a handful of slaves for several months at a time to complete one building. After about 1840, the needs, resources and scale of building in North Carolina had so much increased that important buildings were undertaken by contractors who employed as many as twenty white and black artisans and supervised several projects in several locations at one time. In 1850 there were thirteen contractors, 2474 carpenters, 498 masons and 211 painters and glaziers in North Carolina. In 1860 there were twenty-two contractors, 3217 carpenters, 197 bricklayers and 1320 "mechanics" in the state.[8] The builder N. R. Wood of Lenoir County employed twelve craftsmen in 1858, George Lipscomb of Tarboro employed sixteen workers in 1858, and Ephraim Clayton in Buncombe County employed twenty-eight men in 1850.

In Raleigh, the most important builder was Dabney Cosby.[9] Born in Louisa County, Virginia, in 1779, he trained as a brickmason, built at least four courthouses, two churches, thirteen houses and four college buildings, and supervised the brickwork at Jefferson's University of Virginia, Charlottesville, before moving to North Carolina in 1839. By 1840 Cosby had established himself at Raleigh. His son Dabney, Jr., was also a builder, and his son John Wayt became an architect. Cosby, Sr., was the builder of the Moore County Courthouse at Carthage, 1838–41, City Hall and market, Raleigh, 1840, the "Grecian Doric" Chatham County Courthouse at Pittsboro, 1843–45, and the masonry work for A. J. Davis's additions to Old East and Old West at the University of North Carolina 1845–47. The indefatigable Cosby shared his enthusiasm for building with one of his sons about 1844: "My head has been in a whirlwind for the last 5 weeks. My Co. Ho. & Jail was deliv'd 12th of this month, all Satisfied. . . . I have undertaken the Brick & Plaistering of the 2 College Buildings, C. Hill, each 40 x 42, 4 stories high to be R.C. [roughcast] . . . & have in prospect the Church at Greensboro & a Clerk's office. . . . A jail is to be built at Raleigh this summer which I shall put in for & if the mint is rebuilt I shall [try to do] it."[10] Cosby went on to build A. J. Davis's Presbyterian Church at Chapel Hill, 1847–49, the North Carolina Institution for the Deaf and Dumb, Raleigh, 1847–50, the Yarborough House Hotel, Raleigh, 1849–50, additions to the Governor's Mansion, Raleigh, 1855–56, and the Pitt County Courthouse at Greenville, begun 1858. In 1850, Cosby had enlarged his own house at Dawson and Hargett streets in Raleigh, a two-story brick structure he had owned for a decade, by adding a two-story wing with wide, bracketed eaves and a three-story Italianate tower. This house was demolished in 1954. Cosby died in 1862.

Perhaps the most well-known of all North Carolina builders was John Berry, who was born at Hillsborough in 1798.[11] By 1819 he had become the partner of Samuel Hancock, a local brickmason who may have given Berry his early training. In 1831, when asking for a job, Berry wrote: "I have purchased a number of Books on the science of Building and have made it my study for a number of years back and I flatter myself at this time, from the experience I have had both in practice and theory, that I can have the Building erected in as good stile & as substantially as any other person in this section of country."[12] Berry's own copy of Owen Biddle's influential pattern book *The Young Carpenter's Assistant*, 1805, has survived and is now at the University of North Carolina. Berry was the builder of many of the state's most important buildings, including William Nichols's Masonic Hall at Hillsborough, 1823–25, St. Matthew's Episcopal Church, Hillsborough, 1825–26, St. Luke's Church, Salisbury, 1827–28, the Orange County Courthouse at Hillsborough, 1844–45, A. J. Davis's Alumni Hall at the University of North Carolina, 1850, St. John's College, Oxford, 1855–57, the Hillsborough Military Academy and its Commandant's House, 1859–61. Berry died in 1870.

The most distinctive builder of the era was Jacob W. Holt of Warren County.[13] Born in Prince Edward County, Virginia, in 1811, the son of a carpenter, Holt came to Warren County in the early 1840's. He described himself as a "master mechanic" and employed four slaves and seventeen white craftsmen in 1850. The buildings designed by him have a distinctive Italianate accent, expressed through bold sawwork ornament, paired brackets, paired round-headed windows, central gables and other details which he copied, in simplified form, from pattern books. Holt returned to Virginia after the Civil War and died there in 1880. Holt was the builder of many houses along the border between North Carolina and Virginia in the 1850's.

James F. Post was the most important builder of Wilmington, where he arrived in 1849.[14] He was born in Fairfield, near Caldwell, New Jersey, in 1818. In 1841 he moved to Petersburg, Virginia, and then in October, 1849, he moved to Wilmington. His office ledger, now at the Lower Cape Fear Historical Society, records the work he did between 1849 and 1860, and shows that, as a jack-of-all-work, he was busy putting up shelves, putting down floorcloths, making "ruff cellar steps," fitting locks or building entire houses. Post seems to have made the typical progression from craftsman to designer and was described at his death as "architect and builder." Post was the designer or builder of the Henry Nutt House, 1850, Edward Savage House, 1851, Zebulon Lattimer House, 1852, St. John's Church, 1853–60, City Hall and Thalian Theater, 1855–57, Bellamy Mansion, 1859, First Presbyterian Church, 1859–61, and St. Paul's Lutheran Church, begun in 1859, all at Wilmington. Post was closely associated with builders John C. Wood (1809–73) and his brother Robert B. Wood (1815–90), who came to Wilmington from Massachusetts in 1838. After serving on the Confederate side in the Civil War, Post died at Wilmington in 1899.

Because of its association with the great cathedrals of the Middle Ages, Gothic architecture was often used for ecclesiastical building. St. John's Church, Fayetteville, was begun in June, 1817, and completed in late December, 1818, the first important Gothic church in North Carolina, perhaps designed by William Nichols.[15] The rector, Rev. Gregory I. Bedell, wrote in November, 1818: "The Church . . . owing to the great scarcity of workmen, is not yet finished, but we shall be able to get into it by Christmas. It is built something in the Gothic. . . . It has a fine organ, clock and bell. . . . The chandelier is of sixty lights and cost in Liverpool one hundred guineas."[16] The organ and bell came from New York, the clock from Boston. The church was destroyed by fire in May, 1831, but was immediately rebuilt, incorporating the original walls but without its original clock tower, under the supervision of William Drummond, a builder from Washington who later supervised early construction at the North Carolina Capitol in 1833–34. The second Christ Church at New Bern was built in Gothic Revival style by Martin Stevenson, Thomas S. Gooding and Bennett Flanner, 1821–22, but it burned in 1871.

St. Matthew's Church, Hillsborough, was built by John Berry in 1825–26, and St. Luke's Church, Salisbury, was built in 1827–28, probably by Berry. Both are plain, box-like brick structures with Flemish-bond walls and simple gable roofs, but at both churches the corner brick panels have been decorated with blind lancet arches. A projecting center entrance tower was added to St. Matthew's in 1868–69, and a spire was added in 1875. A tower was added to St. Luke's Church in 1909. None of these early Gothic churches were Romantic creations. They were squarish, symmetrical buildings to which Gothic ornament had merely been applied. St. Mary's Chapel, Hillsborough, 1858–59, is a late example of this simple Gothic village church.

In the second quarter of the 19th century, revival and reform of the Anglican communion encouraged the building of many Gothic Revival parish churches throughout England and America. The old medieval parish churches, built before the Reformation, became models for a holier, less secular kind of religious life and architecture. In place of the boxy, light-filled churches of the 18th century, arranged without chancels so that the people were seated closer to the ritual, the new Gothic Revival churches were intended to be more mysterious, darker and narrower. In his *Essay on Gothic Architecture*, published at Burlington, Vermont, in 1836, John Henry Hopkins, a former parish priest in Pittsburgh and Boston who had become Bishop of Vermont, described the transcendent association which church reformers felt between Gothic design and Christian spirituality: "The multiple perpendicular lines of

The first great Gothic Revival church of North Carolina, St. James, Wilmington, 1839–40, detail from a 19th-century photograph. *Amon Carter Museum, Fort Worth*

buttresses, crowned with pinnacles diminishing to a point, the mullioned windows, and the slender clustered pillars, lead the eye of the beholder upwards . . . in the sky . . . causing, by a kind of physical association, an impression of sublimity more exalted than any other sort of architecture can produce!"[17]

St. James Church, on South Third Street, Wilmington, was the first great Gothic Revival church in North Carolina. On February 7, 1839, the church wardens voted to accept the design of Thomas U. Walter of Philadelphia. Walter (1804–87) had been apprenticed as a master brick-layer, the craft of his father, before working for William Strickland in the 1820's. Walter became most famous as the architect of the gigantic cast-iron dome of the U.S. Capitol. The cornerstone of St. James was laid in April, 1839, construction was supervised by John S. Norris of New York and the new edifice was consecrated in March, 1840. So much more than the country builders' awkward attempts at Gothic design which had preceded his work at St. James, Walter employed tracery, buttresses, crockets, finials, asymmetry and a flexible plan to create a rich and fanciful building. Subsequently St. James lost much of its exterior ornament, notably the pinnacles at the top of its side buttresses, but we can see them in a recently rediscovered early photograph. The sanctuary's ceiling was rebuilt in 1871, and the side galleries were removed in 1889.

Walter also designed the Chapel of the Cross at 304 East Franklin Street, Chapel Hill.[18] Walter's diary records that he made the drawings between September 24 and October 1, 1842, charging $25 for the plan, two elevations and section. William Mercer Green, who had come from Wilmington to be professor of Rhetoric and Belles Lettres at the University, had founded the church—and later supplied the brick used for its construction—and was responsible for the choice of architect. Like St. James, which it imitates in smaller scale, the Chapel of the Cross has a square central entrance tower, a gable roof with crenellations, lancet-arched windows and side and corner buttresses. The Chapel of the Cross was built between 1843 and 1848, its completion long delayed by a lack of money.[19] The church had a metal roof and was painted yellow. The interior walls were painted grey and the woodwork was grained to imitate oak. In 1891 the church was remodelled and a chancel was added.

The First Baptist Church, 239 Middle Street, New Bern, was designed by Thomas and Son of New York in 1846 and completed by July, 1848. Thomas Thomas (1787–1871) was born in Wales and came to New York in 1833. He was a founding member of the American Institution of

Chapel of the Cross, Chapel Hill, drawing by Thomas U. Walter, 1843.
The Athenaeum of Philadelphia

Chapel of the Cross, 304 East Franklin Street, Chapel Hill, 1843–48, late
19th-century photograph. *North Carolina Collection, University of North Carolina*

First Baptist Church, 239 Midde Street, New Bern, 1846–48.

Architects in 1837 and practiced architecture with his son, Griffith Thomas. The First Baptist Church has a central tower, crenellated parapet, corner buttresses, lancet windows and brownstone trim. The interior was remodelled in 1904–07.

Christ Church, 120 East Edenton Street, Raleigh, was designed by the famous Richard Upjohn. The architect's drawings, now at the Avery Library, are dated September 19, 1846. Upjohn (1802–78) came to America from England in 1829 at the age of twenty-seven. Trained as a cabinetmaker, surveyor and draftsman, he worked for the architect Alexander Parris of Boston in the 1830's. Called in to repair and enlarge old Trinity Church, New York, Upjohn designed a completely new structure, a landmark of Gothic Revival church architecture in America, which was built 1844–46. In January, 1846, Bishop L. S. Ives of Raleigh asked Upjohn to design "a neat Gothic church" to seat some six hundred persons and suggested that he adapt the plan of St. Mary's. Burlington, New Jersey, which Upjohn had only recently designed, using a specific 14th-century English church as a model—the first church in America to be specifically copied from an English medieval building.[20] (Ives, born in Connecticut, had been rector of churches in Pennsylvania and New York before coming to North Carolina in 1831, which explains how he knew of Upjohn's work in New York and New Jersey.) In November, 1847, the rector of Christ Church, the Rev. Richard Sharpe Mason, fearing that the church might have to be built of brick rather than stone, begged Upjohn to find a mason in New York who could come to North Carolina to do the stonework: "We are about to spoil your beautiful plan. We find so much difficulty in obtaining a mason whom we can trust!"[21] The mason came from New York and thus Christ Church became the first and only stone Gothic Revival church in North Carolina with a design derived, if secondhand, from an English original. Rev. Mason recognized that Christ Church was something special when he wrote to Upjohn: "The erection of our church will be the means of introducing a new style of church architecture in the South."[22] (Rev. Mason also wrote: "I have been endeavouring to impress upon a lady who talks of building a house in Raleigh to procure a plan from you. We have such villainous barns called houses."[23] Alas, no house by Upjohn was built in North Carolina.) In the fall of 1849, Upjohn sent plans intended for a church to be built at Lexington to John M. Parker of Salisbury, but nothing is known of what became of them.[24]

In 1852 Upjohn published his *Rural Architecture*, a brief but enthusiastic guide to country church-building. He explained how board-and-batten siding—boards laid vertically, their joints covered with thin slats

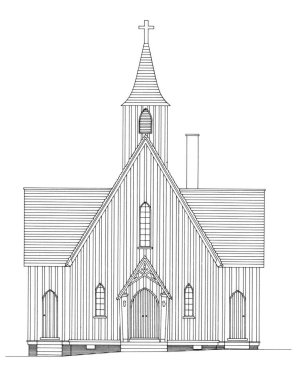

Board-and-batten churches inspired by Upjohn's *Rural Architecture* (New York, 1852): St. Mark's Church, Halifax, 1854–55, top, and St. Mary's Chapel, Raleigh, 1858, bottom.

Christ Church, Raleigh, drawings by Richard Upjohn, 1846. *Avery Library*

Christ Church, 120 East Edenton Street, Raleigh, 1846–48.

Grace Episcopal Church, Plymouth, begun 1860.

or battens—could be used to emphasize the verticality of the Gothic style and do it economically as well. Several board-and-batten carpenter Gothic churches were built in North Carolina during the 1850's, though they seem to have been inspired by, not copied from, Upjohn's designs in *Rural Architecture*: St. Mark's Episcopal Church, King and Church streets, Halifax, 1854–55; St. Paul's Episcopal Church, 209 Ann Street, Beaufort, 1857. But Upjohn was consulted about the construction of the best of these board-and-batten churches, St. Mary's Chapel, Raleigh, 1858.[25]

Grace Episcopal Church, Plymouth, was begun to the designs of Richard Upjohn. In April, 1859, Francis W. Hilliard, the rector, wrote to Upjohn in New York: "Can you give me any exact information with regard to the least cost of a Church . . . supposing that Church to be planned by yourselves? The Church is to be of brick. The ground which it is to occupy is 100 ft. in length. . . . We desire to have a tower . . . upon one corner."[26] Upjohn sent estimates and, later, plans. Construction was begun in August, 1860, and, despite the outbreak of the Civil War, architect and clients continued to correspond harmoniously as late as February, 1861. But only the tower and walls had been completed by 1862, when the Confederates evacuated Plymouth and work on the church ceased. Northern forces used the shell of the church as an asylum for freedmen and government commissary during the war, after which construction was completed using some of the old fabric of Upjohn's church.

Trinity Church, Scotland Neck, was built in 1854–55, to the design of Frank Wills of New York, Wills (1822–56) was born in England, moved to New York by way of Canada in 1847, edited the influential *New York Ecclesiologist* and authored *Ancient English Ecclesiastical Architecture*, 1850. Trinity Church, which was partially destroyed by fire in 1884, is dominated by a tall central tower, with buttresses, pointed-arched windows and crenellated parapet.

Christ Church, at the corner of Church and McMorine streets in Elizabeth City, was built between October, 1856, and December, 1857, to the design of John Crawford Neilson of Baltimore. Neilson (1816–1900) was trained as an engineer and began his career working for railroads. He was the partner of John Rudolph Niernsee from 1848 until 1855, when Niernsee went to South Carolina to supervise construction of the State House at Columbia. Among many projects in Baltimore, they designed six houses in Mt. Vernon Place and several Gothic churches. Christ Church, Elizabeth City, has an asymmetrical tower, lancet windows, corner buttresses and, inside, an open-timbered ceiling.

Trinity Church, Scotland Neck, 1854–55, 19th-century photograph. *Private Collection*

In the fall of 1858, deacons of the First Baptist Church at Wilmington toured Richmond, Baltimore, Washington and other cities, "examining models and consulting architects" for the design of a new church. They selected the Philadelphian Samuel Sloan (1815–84), prolific designer of public buildings and writer of architectural books which were very influential in the 1850's. Born in Pennsylvania, apprenticed as a carpenter and cabinetmaker, Sloan advanced from craftsman to builder and, by 1849, to architect. Construction of the First Baptist Church at Wilmington began in May, 1859. In May, 1860, workmen were laying brick. In June, window frames had been raised on the west side of the building. In August, the walls had risen as high as the gallery. On December 21, the rector, John L. Pritchard, recorded in his diary: "Walked 'round by the church. At work on West side, turning arches over the windows. . . . Heard cannon firing at the news of the secession of South Carolina." Four months later, on April 13, 1861, Rev. Pritchard wrote: "Fort Sumter bombarded all night! . . . Great rejoicing in Wilmington, flag raising, &c. The windows on towers of our church raised to-day." In June, the front gable had been nearly completed, but in July work was halted.[27] The doors and windows were boarded up and lumber piled. The First Baptist Church was finally dedicated in May, 1870. Sloan also designed the First Presbyterian Church in Wilmington, in 1859. It was completed in April, 1861, and burned in 1925.

In the 1840's another kind of Gothic Revival architecture began to make its way from England to America. Scotland's Sir Walter Scott portrayed scenes of heroic medieval pageantry in his novels, popularizing the Gothic world. He built himself a Gothic castle, inspiring copies in America. A reflection of the Romantic movement in all of Western culture, Gothic houses were intended to be private, personal, sentimental and a little bit quirky. A gesture of escape from the growing complexity, urbanization and industrialization of modern life, Romantic buildings were designed for rural and suburban settings. Influenced by the vast American landscape, which had so powerful an impact on painting and literature, Romantic architecture was intended to spring naturally, organically, sympathetically from its pastoral surroundings. Significantly, the Gothic Revival in America first flourished in the Hudson River Valley of New York, a center of landscape painting in the early 19th century. This picturesque movement was popularized by New York's Andrew Jackson Downing, horticulturalist and architectural theorist, in three important works, *A Treatise on the Theory and Practice of Landscape Gardening*, 1841, *Cottage Residences*, 1842, and *The Architecture of Country Houses*, 1850. In May, 1855, Sarah Williams, the wife of a Green County, North Carolina, planter, wrote of her husband and one of her nephews: "Richard thinks of building. Ben purchased Downing's *Architecture* this winter & Richard says he wants us to help him select a plan."[28]

Though the Gothic Revival was in part a reaction against industrialization, elaborate Gothic ornament in wood and metal was facilitated by steam-powered sawmills and iron foundries. It is fascinating to note that Romanticism and industrialization, so apparently antithetical, came to England at the same time, the end of the 18th century, and developed side by side as the two most important factors of 19th-century English life. Perhaps the South's industrial backwardness was one reason why the Gothic Revival was used less often in that region than in the Northeast and Midwest. The greatest popularizer of the Gothic Revival in America, New York's Alexander Jackson Davis, was active in North Carolina between 1832 and 1860. It is significant that in North Carolina he more often employed the simpler Tuscan style, which was easier to build, and that not one of his Gothic Revival designs was ever executed in North Carolina, though they survive in Davis's beautiful drawings. Except for Davis's work (discussed in the following chapter), only two important examples of domestic Gothic Revival design are known in the state. The Dr. James B. Hughes House, which once stood on Broad Street in New Bern, has been demolished. Though it had some of the embellishments of the Gothic—crenellated parapet, castellated main entrance, Tudor arches and angle turrets—it was really a conventional mid 19th-century house in a fancy costume. In Wilmington, master builder James Post constructed a Gothic "castle" for Donald MacRae in 1850, also now demolished.

Dr. James B. Hughes House, New Bern, undocumented, in an 1864 photograph. *North Carolina Collection, University of North Carolina*

In these works, the symmetrical, mostly white, houses of the neoclassic period were replaced by informal, asymmetrical, earth-colored villas of the Romantic era. Roofs became steeply pitched gables, with extended eaves and decorated bargeboards. Rooflines were further enlivened with clustered tall chimney stacks, towers, crenellated parapets, finials and crocket ornaments. Facades were embellished with trellised verandahs, clustered columns, bay and oriel windows, Tudor, ogee or pointed arches, stone tracery and corner buttresses with weatherings. Interiors were decorated with plaster vaults, leaded stained glass, drip mouldings and foliated ornament. James Johnston's wonderful octagonal library at Hayes, outside Edenton, may have been designed by William Nichols in 1815–17 or added later, perhaps in 1839, when improvements were made on the property.[29] David Paton, architect of the North Carolina Capitol during the late 1830's, intended to design

Library at Hayes, Edenton, documentation uncertain.

Library at North Carolina Capitol, Raleigh, 1841–42.

North Carolina Institution for the Deaf and Dumb, Raleigh, 1848–50, mid-19th century woodcut. *North Carolina Collection, University of North Carolina*

Gothic rooms for the State Library and Supreme Court. He had already ordered Gothic mantels from John Struthers of Philadelphia before he left Raleigh in 1840 and promised to send drawings for these rooms but apparently never did. The State Library was completed between late 1841 and the spring of 1842 by carpenters P. and W. Conrad of Lexington. The Supreme Court was completed by July, 1841, but, after the room was turned over to the state geologist, a Gothic gallery, made of poplar, was added by carpenters Thomas Briggs and James Dodd in 1857–58.[30]

Gothic Revival design, so fitting an expression for the spiritual world of churches and the intellectual world of libraries, was also favored for schools and military buildings. The Institution for the Deaf and Dumb at Raleigh opened in rented rooms with seven students in May, 1845. The cornerstone of a new Gothic building was laid in April, 1848, and it was occupied in January, 1849, though still incomplete. Though the general plan had been devised by William D. Cook, the school's principal, the exterior was designed by John Wayt Cosby, whose father, Dabney, was its builder.[31] The basement contained dining room, storerooms and kitchen. The first story contained library, reception room, parlor, sitting room, workrooms, clothing storerooms. The second story contained apartments for the principal and matron, principal's office, pupils' rooms, guest rooms. The third story had teachers' bedrooms and two hospital rooms. The main block was four stories high, sixty feet by thirty-six feet, with two three-story wings, each twenty-two by thirty-eight feet.[32] In 1852 the school had sixty-eight pupils. The building was remodelled in 1899 and finally demolished in 1953.

St. John's College at Oxford was founded by the Masons to provide free education for poor boys. The cornerstone of this commanding Gothic Revival structure was laid in June, 1855, and it was completed in 1857. The school operated for a brief period before the Civil War, after which it became an orphanage, which chose to demolish the original building in 1955. It was a four-story brick structure, with a tall square central tower, tiers of pointed and circular windows with drip mouldings, and two shorter octagonal towers. John Berry of Hillsborough supervised the brickwork and Jacob Holt of Warrenton supervised the carpentry. The building was 122 feet long and 40 feet wide and contained fifty-three dormitory rooms, a chapel, and recitation and social halls.

The North Carolina Military Institute at Charlotte was founded by Daniel Harvey Hill, a professor at nearby Davidson College. Its cornerstone was laid in 1858 and the building was completed in 1859, with

St. John's College, Oxford, 1855–57, center of front exterior. *St. John's College*

The possible model for the Commandant's House at Hillsborough Military Academy, 1858–60, may have been Plate LX of Samuel Sloan's *Model Architect* (Philadelphia, 1852). *Private Collection*

Kilburn-Guion House, New Bern, undocumented, seen in an 1864 photograph. *North Carolina Collection, University of North Carolina*

three pavilions, their gables facing forward with crenellated parapets, corner towers and drip mouldings. The main building of Greensboro Female College was built in 1845 and wings were added in 1857 and 1861, with a central portico and crenellated pediments. The design for the Pitt County Courthouse, made by Jacob Holt or his brother Thomas Holt in 1858, had Gothic towers, turrets and buttresses.

The Hillsborough Military Academy was founded in February, 1858, by Charles Courtney Tew, born in Charleston and a graduate of the Citadel in Charleston. The building was completed in 1860. The three-story school building was brick, laid in Flemish bond, with crenellated parapets, 215 feet long. Its central entrance was marked by two engaged round towers and raised parapet with lancet windows. The design was by John A. Kay of Columbia, South Carolina. The military school closed in 1868, and the school building was demolished in 1938. The nearby commandant's house still stands, however. It has crenellated parapet, a central mock-Gothic window and exotic corner towers. All of the windows, except those on the generally shaded north side, are equipped with interior shutters which slide into wall pockets.

Of the Romantic styles, the Italianate became the most popular, primarily because it was far easier to build than the Gothic. Inspired by the rural architecture of the north Italian countryside, the Italian Villa style was first employed conspicuously by John Nash in Regency England. A. J. Downing published both Italian villas and Gothic castles in his books of the late 1840's and 1850's. Italian villas were generally asymmetrical in plan, with a tall tower and arcaded porch and bay windows. Roofs were low, with wide overhanging eaves, supported by brackets, with a cupola or lantern. Round-headed windows were often grouped in twos and threes and embellished with heavy hood mouldings or pediments. Not surprisingly, sophisticated Charlestonians were responsible for an early Italianate design in North Carolina. Since the 1830's, South Carolinians had fled during the steamy summer months from the miasmal low-country to the North Carolina mountain resort of Flat Rock. It was there in 1852–54 that Charleston architect Edward C. Jones virtually rebuilt the small Church of St. John-in-the-Wilderness, adding the characteristic splayed eaves, decorated bargeboards, round-headed windows and asymmetrical tower.

Especially in North Carolina, where the design as well as the construction of so many important buildings was left to self-taught master builders, the greatest force behind the spread of Romantic styles was architectural books. Handbooks of the 18th and early 19th centuries had been mostly illustrated dictionaries, with pictures of the classical orders, solu-

Commandant's House, Hillsborough Military Academy, 1858–60.

tions to geometrical problems of stair, wall and roof structure, a few sample doors, windows and chimneypieces, and elevations and plans for two or three model houses and a church. But by the mid-19th century, books showed country builders elaborate plans, perspective views, interior details for many different kinds of buildings in various styles—Greek, Italian, Gothic or Persian—all specific and complete, with suggestions for landscaping, painting, furnishing and costs.

One of the most influential mid-century pattern books used in North Carolina was William H. Ranlett's *The Architect*, published in 1847. Wessington, a French-inspired villa at 120 West King Street in Edenton, was built for Dr. Thomas D. Warren about 1851. Dr. Warren owned a copy of Ranlett's book (that copy, bearing his signature, is preserved by descendants) and must have instructed a builder to copy the general scheme, as well as roof, columns, cornice, chimneys, doors, windows and balustrades, of his Design XX, but enlarging the porch and balconies and adding dormers.

Jacob Holt, the prominent builder in Warren County, copied many details, in simplified form, from Ranlett's book, particularly its Design XVIII. Holt derived the design of his own house, built in Warrenton about 1855, from Design I of *The Model Architect*, another influential architectural book, by Samuel Sloan of Philadelphia, published in 1852. That particular design Sloan seems to have copied himself from A. J. Downing's *Cottage Residences*, though it had actually originated with John Notman of Philadelphia.

Cooleemee, an "Anglo-Grecian villa" near the Yadkin River and town of Advance, was built between 1853 and 1855 for Peter Wilson Hairston. The builders, the Conrad brothers of Lexington, copied a plan and decorative details from Design X of Ranlett's book. Jeb Stuart, the future Confederate general and brother of Hairston's first wife, wrote to the owner in August, 1854: "I take pleasure in informing you that 'all's right' at Cooleemee Hill. Your house is progressing rapidly. The brick has risen more than half way up the 2d story window and door frames. In fact from my observation I am a little apprehensive . . . that they are going too fast, that the quantity was disproportionate with the quality of the work, for the interior joists of masonry were not as carefully filled and as accurately adjusted as principles of Civil Engineering require."[33] Cooleemee has a cruciform plan with an octagonal central hall, lit by a glazed cupola, and a remarkable spiral stair. The exterior has a low gabled roof, dentil eaves cornice, an Ionic porch on the west and a Doric porch on the east.

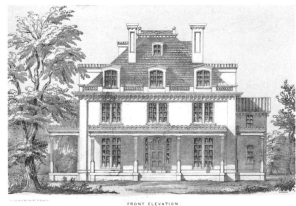

FRONT ELEVATION.

PERSPECTIVE VIEW.

Top: Wessington, 120 West King Street, Edenton, c. 1851, with its model, Design XX of William H. Ranlett's *The Architect* (New York, 1847). Bottom: Jacob Holt House, Warrenton, c. 1855, with its model, Design I of Samuel Sloan's *The Model Architect* (Philadelphia, 1852). *Holt photograph from North Carolina Archives and History, book illustrations from private collection*

Cooleemee, Advance vicinity, 1853–55, with, opposite, its model, Design X of
Ranlett's *The Architect*, a sectional view and plan. *Photograph by Frances Benjamin
Johnston, Library of Congress, Sloan illustration from private collection*

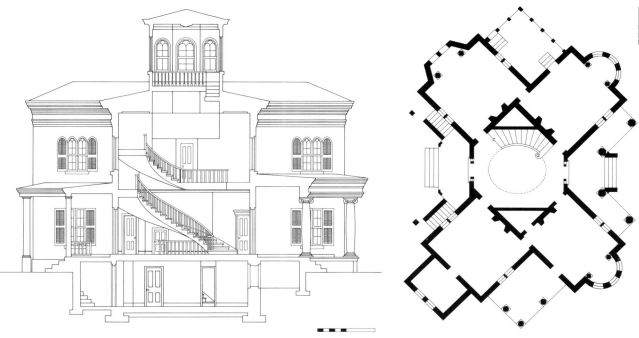

Cooleemee, stairhall.

Sloan designed the First Baptist and the First Presbyterian churches at Wilmington in the late 1850's. In fact, his work in North Carolina was so considerable that he moved his office from Philadelphia to Raleigh in the mid-1870's. Few of Sloan's personal and professional papers have survived. He may have designed Rose Villa, an Italianate house built at Greensboro about 1852 for Alexander P. Eckel, a Tennessee-born merchant, jeweler, druggist and first mayor of Greensboro. Rose Villa, which burned in 1881, was a two-story, stuccoed brick structure with a four-story, balconied, asymmetrical tower, wide bracketed eaves and paired, round-headed windows and bay windows. The design closely

Rose Villa, Greensboro, c. 1852, and similar design, Figure 23, in Samuel Sloan's *Homestead Architecture* (Philadelphia, 1861). *Photograph from Greensboro Historical Museum, Sloan illustration from Avery Library*

resembles Figure 23 ("the country-seat of a man of ample fortune") of Sloan's *Homestead Architecture*, published in 1861, which also illustrates one of his most famous Southern buildings, Longwood at Natchez, Mississippi. Sloan may have designed Dunleith, built for Judge Robert P. Dick of Greensboro about 1856. The house was demolished in 1968. A frame structure, with flanking gables facing forward over the side bays, the design is related to Design XXXI of Sloan's *The Model Architect*, which also inspired Jacob Holt. The front entrance had columns and floral spandrels cast in iron. Some of Sloan's post-Civil War projects in North Carolina included additions to A. J. Davis's Insane Asylum at Raleigh, 1875, the Western North Carolina Insane Asylum at Morganton, 1875–86, a school at New Bern, 1883–85, a gymnasium and ballroom at the University of North Carolina, 1883–84. Sloan suffered a stroke at Morganton and died in July, 1884.[34]

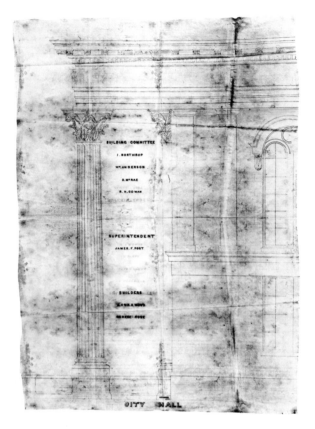

Town Hall and Thalian Theater, Wilmington, drawing of portico and flank elevation by R. B. Wood, 1855. *City of Wilmington*

The Town Hall and Thalian Theater at North Third and Princess streets in Wilmington was designed by John Trimble of New York with the assistance of James Post and the Wood brothers.[35] Trimble was the designer of some forty theaters, most of them in New York. Post was hired to make the working plans in November, 1855, and then was paid $4 a day for general supervision. Robert Wood was hired to design a new, larger portico for the City Hall front. (A drawing signed "R.B. Wood, 1855" has been found in the building's cornerstone.) Construction was begun in November, 1855, and completed in October, 1858. The Thalian Theater seated 1200–1500 persons, its ceiling, walls and proscenium arch were "handsomely frescoed," a decorative stage curtain was painted by Russell Smith of Philadelphia, the hall was lit by gas, and stage machinery was designed by Joseph Walker of Philadelphia. Another building which is mostly classical in detail but Romantic in spirit is the Davidson County Courthouse, at Main and Center streets in Lexington, constructed by local builders Dudley and Ashley in 1857–58, with a heroic prostyle Roman Corinthian portico and octagonal bell tower. Dr. John Bellamy's mansion at 503 Market Street in Wilmington was built by James Post to the designs of Rufus Bunnell of Vermont in 1859. Like the Town Hall and Thalian Theater and the Davidson Courthouse, the exterior of Bellamy's mansion is an extravagant assemblage of classical and Italianate details—a Palladian window, pedimented entrance, cupola, Corinthian capitals and cornice, peripteral colonnade and round-headed windows—all creating a restlessly Romantic effect. The restoration of this building, after a devastating fire, seems unlikely.

Another practitioner of this Romantic classicism was William Percival, who came to Raleigh from England by way of Richmond, where he was principal of the design department of the Virginia Mechanics Institute, in the late 1850's.[36] After designing the First Baptist Church, a Gothic Revival structure facing the Capitol Square in Raleigh, in 1857, Percival set up an office in the North Carolina capital in 1858. "With an Educational Training and a thorough Practical Experience of more than sixteen years," as he described himself, Percival was the most accomplished resident architect in North Carolina in the mid-19th century.[37] A traveller who sat beside him on a stagecoach in 1858 described Percival as "this portly gentleman at my side . . . a man of learning, taste and ability."[38] Percival was an eclectic designer who equipped most of his buildings with the latest modern conveniences—hot air furnaces, gas lights, hot and cold running water and water closets. He favored Italianate designs, sandstone trim, domed rotundas, Corinthian capitals and shallow porches.

Town Hall and Thalian Theater, North Third and Princess streets, Wilmington, 1855–58, a 19th-century view. *North Carolina Collection, University of North Carolina*

Courthouse, Main and Center streets, Lexington, 1857–58.

Dr. John Bellamy House, 503 Market Street, Wilmington, 1859.

Calvary Episcopal Church, Tarboro, design by William Percival, 1860. *Calvary Episcopal Church*

The villa which Percival designed for Rufus Sylvester Tucker, a twenty-eight-year-old merchant, in Raleigh, was demolished in 1968. We know its exterior appearance, however, from photographs: a two-story brick structure with a three-story corner tower, central gable, wide, bracketed eaves, paired, round-headed windows, decorative window canopies and arcaded porches supported by paired colonettes. The house was equipped with hot air furnace, gas lights, cold and hot running water and second-story bathrooms. The walls and ceilings were decorated by a German painter, Augustus Freund. A second Raleigh villa was begun in 1858 for the wealthy, gregarious and extravagant William Montford Boylan. Completed two years later, it was another Italianate design with wide bracketed eaves, central gable, cupola and shallow porches supported by paired colonettes. Inside, the capitals of the columns of the rotunda depict squirrels and birds in place of the usual Corinthian foliated ornament, and window shutters slide into wall pockets. A third villa in Raleigh was designed in 1859 for Carter B. Harrison, a railroad investor who was preparing to marry for the first time at the advanced age of forty-one. Demolished in 1967, this house had Percival's characteristic cupola, round-headed windows, decorative window hoods and heavy mouldings, and porches with paired colonettes.

In the prosperous town of Tarboro, Percival designed another villa for William S. Battle, a cotton mill owner and planter, at 1100 Albemarle Avenue in 1858. It was completed in 1861. The visitor crosses a stone-paved vestibule into a rotunda lit by a stained-glass skylight. Percival also designed the Calvary Episcopal Church at Tarboro in the Gothic Revival style. Work on the church was suspended in 1861, after the walls, roof, floor and spire had been constructed, and the church was not completed until 1867. In September, 1858, Percival had exhibited "Working Drawings in detail and full specifications" for the Caswell County Courthouse at Yanceyville, which was completed in 1861. The complicated design of the Courthouse includes an octagonal clock tower, heavy modillion cornice, corbelled brick arcading and round-headed windows. The polychromed cast-iron capitals depict ears of corn and tobacco leaves. Percival also designed the First Baptist Church at Hillsborough in 1860, a Romanesque edifice, and the New East and New West buildings at the University of North Carolina in 1858–59. He also did other unidentified work for Robert Norfleet of Tarboro and Kenelm J. Lewis of Nash County before returning to Virginia in 1860.

While Percival's villas have been demolished or lost much of their original character, it is fortunate that one great Italian villa by another accomplished designer has survived, for the most part, in splendid, origi-

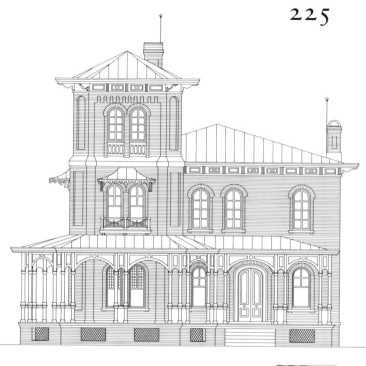

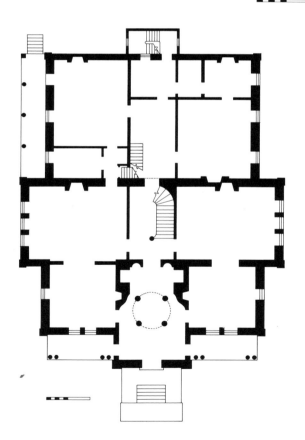

Top: Rufus Sylvester Tucker House, Raleigh, 1858, with front elevation. *North Carolina Archives and History*. Bottom: William Montford Boylan House, Raleigh, 1858, with its plan.

William Montford Boylan House, hall.

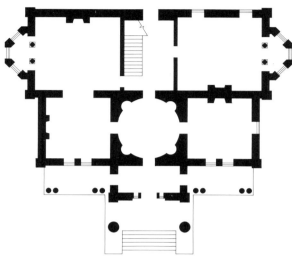

Top: William S. Battle House, 1100 Albemarle Avenue, Tarboro, 1858, with its plan.
Bottom: Carter B. Harrison House, Raleigh, 1859. *North Carolina Archives and History*

nal condition. Coolmore, the home of Dr. Joseph Powell, about four miles east of Tarboro, was built between 1857 and 1860 to the design of Edmund G. Lind, an English-born architect working in Baltimore. Lind was born in London in 1829 and began the study of architecture in 1847. After apprenticeship in London, Lind sailed to American in October, 1855, and soon settled in Baltimore, where he worked in the office of Nathan G. Starkweather and later formed a partnership with William T. Murdoch. This partnership was, however, short-lived, for, according to Lind's daughter, Murdoch "drank and did no work." Lind's own catalogue of his works, preserved at the Maryland Historical Society, lists some fifteen projects—houses, stores, churches, courthouses, a school and restaurant—undertaken at Tarboro and Wilson, North Carolina, between 1858 and 1861.[39] During the administration of President U. S. Grant, Lind was a principal designer of U.S. government buildings. He died in 1909.[40]

Coolmore, Dr. Joseph Powell House, Tarboro, mid-19th century lithograph. *Private Collection*

Coolmore, the first and most important of Lind's works in North Carolina, is a two-story frame house with one-story wings, a copper-clad roof, decorative gables, a cupola, wide, bracketed eaves and round-headed windows in pairs. A lithograph, showing Lind's original design, suggests that Coolmore was intended to be a brick, stuccoed structure, but that Dr. Powell executed it as a frame, weatherboarded building. A visitor enters a semicircular hall, with walls ornamented by pilasters on pedestals, Corinthian capitals and cornice, all highlighted with blue

Coolmore, Tarboro, entrance hall.

Coolmore, stair.

marbleizing and gilt decoration. Beyond, the visitor proceeds to an oval stair hall which ascends to a cupola, with niches, painted floorcloths and trompe l'oeil painting. Several rooms retain their original carpets, curtains and furnishings, most of which were ordered from Baltimore in the summer of 1860. The house was lit by its own coal gasworks, and water was piped to a copper-lined wooden tank in the attic.

Orson Squire Fowler (1809–87) was a phrenologist, vegetarian, teetotaler, sex educator and publisher whose exotic, quixotic architectural ideas appealed to the emotional and idealistic age in which he lived. In his treatise, *A Home for All, or the Gravel Wall and Octagon Mode of Building*, 1853, Fowler looked to the natural world for his building ideas. Like nature's own favorite shapes—fruits, eggs, nuts, seeds and tree trunks—Fowler believed that houses should be circular—or, next best, octagonal—in plan. He promised that octagonal buildings would be "several hundred percent" cheaper than any others. Similarly, walls should be erected with nature's own building materials—lime, stone and sand—which would be "simple, durable, easily applied, everywhere abundant, easily rendered beautiful, comfortable and every way complete." Singlehandedly, Fowler popularized a new style of domestic building in America. However, it was only a passing fad, for these octagonal buildings were architectural mules, without legitimate ancestry or hope of offspring.

Dr. William T. Sparrow, a physician who had gone to California in an unsuccessful search for gold in 1849, used Fowler's book as the model for his octagonal house, The Inkwell, which was built in the vicinity of Englehard on the North Carolina coast about 1857.[41] Sparrow, a skilled carpenter who probably learned that craft in his father's shipyard as a child, may have built the house himself. The plan, exterior and other details were copied from Design 41 of *A Home for All*, an octagonal cottage planned by Morgan and Brothers of Williamsburg, New York, for Fowler's engraver, William Howland. Like that scheme, The Inkwell had paired windows (some of which are blind, because they face closet walls), a central chimney serving twin parlors, which are flanked by a hall on one side and closets on the other. Sparrow also followed Fowler's advice by installing wooden, tin-lined gutters to carry water from the cedar-shingled roof to a cistern and by employing an unusual method of board-wall construction which used interleaved, horizontal planks. Another octagonal house, Cedar Point, was built for Edward Hill in Carteret County, three miles east of Swansboro in 1855. Hill's house roughly follows Figure 13 of *A Home for All*, with a central hall flanked on each side by a square room and two triangular rooms.

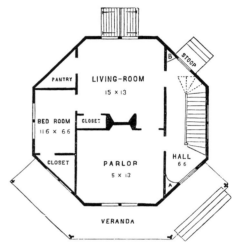

The Inkwell, Dr. William T. Sparrow House, Englehard vicinity, c. 1857, with its model, the plan and elevation of Design 41 in Fowler's *A Home for All* (New York, 1853). *Fowler illustrations from private collection*

Cedar Point, Edward Hill House, Swansboro
vicinity, 1855, 19th-century photograph.
North Carolina Archives and History

Another exercise at architectural polygony is the house that Philip Sowers began outside the present-day hamlet of Churchland in 1860. With an amazing Y-shaped plan, the house is actually deodecagonal! The house was finished about 1866, with distinctive walnut woodwork attributed to the local craftsman Henry Grubb.[42]

A later, but irresistible, sequel to these geometric buildings was Harriet Irwin's design for hexagonal houses, which she patented in 1869 under the sexless signature of "H. M. Irwin."[43] She was born in Mecklenberg County in 1828, the daughter of a Presbyterian minister who served as the first president of Davidson College. An invalid, Irwin lived in Charlotte between 1852 and her death in 1897. In her patent application, she wrote: "The objects of my invention are the economizing of space and building-materials, the obtaining of economical heating mediums, thorough lighting and ventilation, and facilities for inexpensive ornamentation." No space would be wasted with unnecessary passageways, there would be plentiful light and air in every room, and lozenge-shaped chambers would enclose more useful area with the expenditure of less material, labor and money than conventional rectangular rooms. Between 1869 and 1871, Irwin, with her husband and brother, built and sold hexagonal houses in Charlotte, one of which stood at 612 West 5th Street until its demolition in 1965. In 1871, Irwin published a curious novel, *The Hermit of Patraea*, which tells the story of a sickly young man who travels to the wilderness of Arabia and meets a hermit. The hermit warns against the dangers of "artificial food, artificial heat and artificial light" and introduces him to the virtues of organic, natural and healthy living—and to six-sided dwellings. The young man returns to civilization—and becomes an architect of six-sided buildings!

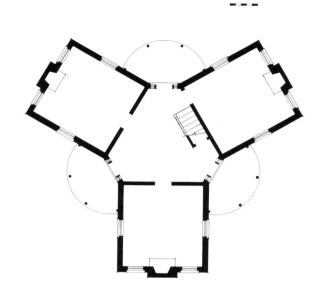

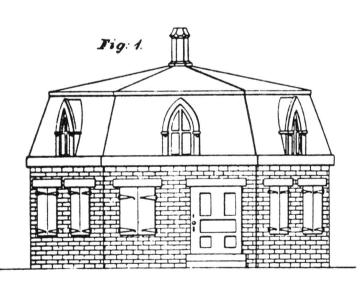

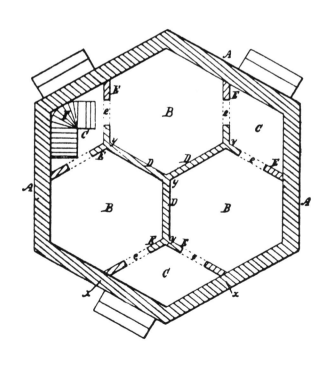

Top: Philip Sowers House, Churchland vicinity, begun 1860, with its plan. *Plan by Martin Meek*. Bottom: H. M. Irwin's design for a hexagonal house, 1869. *U.S. Patent Office*

VI. *A. J. Davis*
in North Carolina

"I have consulted an Architect, Mr. A. J. Davis. . . . He is thoroughly acquainted with his Business, can give Designs for exteriors & also for interior arrangements for Libraries, & Busts & Nooks for Art, for Gates, &c., &c. . . . He will either furnish a Design, with working Drawings & ample Specifications for the proper execution of the work or superintend the Erection." Robert Donaldson, a graduate of the University of North Carolina who had established himself as a prosperous commission merchant and patron of the arts in New York in the late 1820's, was writing in 1843 to David L. Swain, the young President of the University who had asked Donaldson to recommend an architect for campus improvements. "Mr. Davis," Donaldson wrote, "is the readiest & most skillful Draughtsman that I know. In fact, the Danger is, when he mounts the Pegasus of Design . . . there might be too much temptation held out by his fertile inventions & suggestions!"[1] Though Davis had done some sporadic work in North Carolina since 1832, this generous introduction began seventeen years of more active effort. Important to Davis and even more important to North Carolina, these works illuminate Davis's career and the evolving practice of architecture as a profession in America.[2]

Alexander Jackson Davis was born in New York in 1803, the son of a religious publisher. After working as a printer, young Davis turned to architectural drawing. In 1827 and 1828 he made two long trips to Boston, where he sketched and studied architecture. At the Boston Athenaeum Davis discovered Stuart and Revett's *Antiquities of Athens*. Later Davis wrote that he dated the start of his professional architectural career from March 15, 1828, the day he first saw those volumes. In 1829, at the age of twenty-six, Davis became the partner of Ithiel Town, the rich and famous designer of wooden truss bridges and roofs. The Town and Davis partnership lasted until 1835 and was resumed briefly in 1842–43. In the early 1830's they submitted designs for the new State Capitol at Raleigh.

Davis, who called himself an "architectural composer," approached architecture as an artist. At the start of his career, John Trumbull encouraged his painting skills and Rembrandt Peale encouraged him to concentrate on architectural drawing. Davis, who never had an opportunity to make an academic study of architecture or travel abroad to see world architecture firsthand, collected scrapbooks of prints and drawings which illustrated Grecian, Roman, Egyptian and Gothic designs and provided ideas for details he could use in his work. Though Davis would design and superintend construction of a building for a commission, he also offered what we might call today mail-order architecture. For $10 he would provide drawings for a church of moderate size, while drawings of a house would cost from $50 to $150. For $30 he would provide general designs, without working drawings, for a simple farm house, for $25 a lodge or garden building, for $15 the front elevation of a house, for $15 an entrance gate with a section of adjoining fence. For $5 Davis would answer architectural inquiries, in person or by mail.[3] Davis worked alone for most of his career, doing all the drafting himself. Because his production was so limited, Davis would have been far less influential had his work not been so widely published. But Davis became one of the most important tastemakers of 19th century America when his drawings were used by Andrew Jackson Downing, horticulturalist and architectural theorist, in three landmark works, *A Treatise on the Theory and Practice of Landscape Gardening*, 1841, *Cottage Residences*, 1842, and *The Architecture of Country Houses*, 1850.

Robert Donaldson was one of the most important early patrons of Davis, Downing and Town.[4] In 1831, after a fire ravaged Fayetteville, Town and Davis designed, without charge, a new Presbyterian Church to replace one that had been destroyed, a courtesy to Donaldson, who was a native of Fayetteville and a devout Presbyterian.[5] The drawings were made in October, 1831, and the church opened in August, 1832. (One of the drawings, of the church's roof truss, "Designed by A. J. Davis on the principle of I. Town's," is now at the Metropolitan Museum.) Then, in the fall of 1832, Donaldson, a graduate of the University of North Carolina, asked Davis to prepare plans and estimates for a hall for the Philanthropic Society, a student organization at the University to which he and his brother James had belonged. In October, Davis prepared elevations, sections and detailed specifications for a forty-foot square "Doric building," but it was not built, because of lack of funds.[6] Meanwhile, in New York, Davis designed for Donaldson a Gothic castle at Fishkill in 1834 and renovations to Blithewood, his country house overlooking the Hudson, in 1836. In 1837 Davis presented the first copy

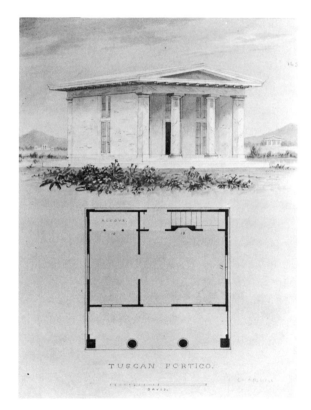

Design for a Tuscan temple, probably the "Doric building" for the Philanthropic Society, Chapel Hill, 1832, by A. J. Davis. *Metropolitan Museum of Art, Harris Brisbane Dick Fund, 24.66.1401(165)*

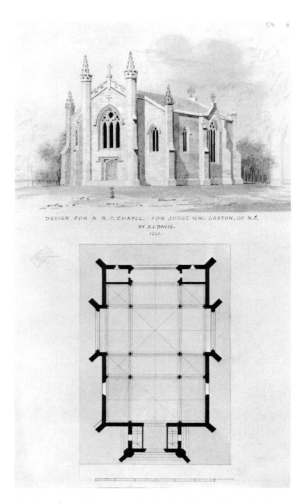

Design for a Roman Catholic Chapel for Judge Gaston, c. 1840, by A. J. Davis. *Metropolitan Museum of Art, Harris Brisbane Dick Fund, 24.66.1403(34)*

of his publication, *Rural Residences*, to Donaldson, who probably introduced Davis to Andrew Jackson Downing. In 1842 Downing dedicated his *Cottage Residences*, with illustrations by Davis, to Donaldson, whom he called "Arbiter elegantiarum."

William Gaston was a Princeton-educated lawyer, state legislator, Congressman and justice of the North Carolina Supreme Court. He was also Ithiel Town's lawyer in North Carolina and the father-in-law of Robert Donaldson. (In November, 1833, Davis made a view of the new North Carolina Capitol, which Ithiel Town intended to present to Gaston, probably a token of thanks for Gaston's efforts to get that important commission for the new firm of Town and Davis.) Gaston was the most prominent Catholic in North Carolina, at a time when the state constitution required officeholders to be not only Christians but Protestants as well! According to tradition, the first Catholic mass in North Carolina had been celebrated in Gaston's house in May, 1821. In June, 1834, Davis made two drawings for a Catholic chapel for Gaston, to be built at New Bern.[7] However, the moment was inopportune—Gaston was defending the appointment of Catholics to government office—and the church was not built. Later, Davis made another drawing for a larger Catholic church for Gaston, and, after Gaston's death in 1844, Davis designed a sarcophagus for Gaston's grave.[8]

When David L. Swain, who had been the youngest governor in North Carolina's history, became President of the University of North Carolina in 1836, the campus was a disorderly cluster of seven box-like buildings. The college had opened in 1795. Three gable-roofed brick buildings faced a clearing in the forest—an East Building of 1793, a South Building of 1798–1814 and a West Building of 1822–27. These contained dormitories for 130 students, three recitation halls, library, laboratory and rooms for two literary societies. Two smaller brick buildings, Person Hall, 1797, and Gerrard Hall, 1822–37, were used for assemblies and worship. There were also two small frame buildings—the President's House and a steward's hall. There were only nine faculty members, including the President who doubled as Professor of Law, but the college was rapidly outgrowing the old buildings.

Swain, whose taste for architecture and building had probably been stimulated by his participation while he was Governor in construction of the new State Capitol at Raleigh, now set about improving the University. He ordered erection of rock walls 'round the campus, to keep out the cattle, hogs and sheep which wandered in from the nearby village. Following instructions provided by David Paton, one of the architects of the Capitol, Swain tried to dress up the old University buildings by roughcasting their plain brick walls. Swain wrote in March, 1840: "We are . . . about to change the dull aspect of the college edifices by covering them with a preparation made of equal quantities of Roman Cement, and common mustard lime, with the addition of one-tenth sulphuric acid, to the quantity of water with which they are mixed."[9]

At Donaldson's urging, President Swain now invited Davis to travel to Chapel Hill to advise him on enlargements to the University. In January, 1844, along with the University's draft for travel expenses, Donaldson sent Davis some free advice: "With respect to the contemplated Buildings at the University, you must take into consideration the materials & mechanics there. My opinion decidedly is to build the Society Halls of Brick & to stucco them. Durability, safety from fire, elegance of exterior, economy in the Columns, &c. will be thereby obtained. . . . You had better leave complete designs for the interiors of the Library & Halls . . . Book cases, brackets & pedestals for Busts (& some ornamental Works of Art) of Philosophers, Globes, Maps, &c., &c."[10] On January 23, Davis left New York and, travelling by railroad and stage through Washington, Richmond, Petersburg, Blakely and Raleigh, reached Chapel Hill on January 31.[11] Davis examined the buildings and grounds of the University and made plans for extending the old East and West Buildings at their northern ends and improving the old South Building and chapel, Gerrard Hall.[12] On February 2, Davis met the faculty and immediately began sketching preliminary plans which he presented to the trustees on February 19. He showed the trustees plans for landscaping, entrance gates, terraces, shrubbery and a botanic garden.[13] This was only the first of some nine reports which Davis would present to the trustees over the next sixteen years.

Additions to the north ends of the old East and West Buildings would provide space for more dormitory rooms, meeting halls (Davis called them "Odeons")[14] for the two literary societies and dome-lit libraries. Four gigantic pilasters at the gable end of each building would create the impression of a pedimented temple and lend a monumental orderliness to the view of the University's haphazardly arranged buildings as seen from the village. In the tall, narrow, three-story space between the central pilasters of each temple-like end, Davis placed an entrance door and windows, unified visually with recessed panels and dark paint colors. This arrangement of doors and windows, sometimes pairs of windows, usually set between pilasters, treated as a single vertical shaft, Davis called "Davisean windows." Davis explained the design to President Swain in March, 1845: "The whole space between the two pilasters is to be filled with plain sunk panel, like the door, and to be the same plane

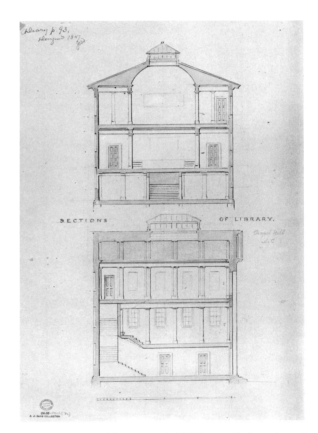

Additions to Old East and Old West, University of North Carolina, Chapel Hill, sectional views by A. J. Davis, c. 1844. *Metropolitan Museum of Art, Harris Brisbane Dick Fund, 24.66.1406(74 verso)*

(flush) with the opening part; the glazed part without side or lintel, other than those panels above and below, which come against the beams; and the whole is to look like the door. . . . No part of the surface, from top to bottom, is to project over but be in one uniform plane, in front, surrounded by a bold architrave, as per plan, rising to the top of the pilasters." He continued his lecture on aesthetics: "By panelling the whole space between the pilasters of N. front we may pierce any of the panels for light. Besides, we would give a commonplace character by inserting ordinary factory-like windows, wholly at variance with the other features of this front, which I wish to preserve in a grave or august character, even at the hazard of a contrast with the sides of the building. The trees will shut out the two contrasting faces, in a great degree." Then Davis concluded ruefully, likening the one good view of these buildings to the limited vision of the mythological Cyclops: "And if they should not, it will be better (in my mind) that the buildings have one redeeming characteristic feature—one good eye, altho' that be Cyclopean in its character!"[15] Foundations were laid for these additions in February, 1845, and the buildings were completed in 1847.[16] The old and new structures were joined with a new, bracketed roof, but an obvious break in the masonry is clearly visible.

Left: Old East, seen in a mid-19th century lithograph. Right: Old West, seen in a 19th-century photograph. *North Carolina Collection, University of North Carolina*

On February 3, 1844, after his meeting with the University trustees, Davis rode by carriage to Greensboro with John Motley Morehead, a schoolmate of Robert Donaldson at the University and a member of its building committee. Morehead, a Virginian who had moved to North Carolina in 1798, was a lawyer, state legislator, Governor, 1840–44, and would become first president of the North Carolina Railroad. Morehead lived at Greensboro in a simple frame house of the 1790's which he had purchased and enlarged in the late 1820's. Now Davis examined the Governor's property, called Blandwood, and devised further enlargements.[17] In front of the old house, completely obscuring it from view, Davis planned a wide-eaved, bracketed Italian villa with central three-story tower and covered passageways leading to flanking dependencies. Many of the windows and interior shutters were designed to slide into the wall pockets.[18]

Davis spent two weeks with Governor Morehead in Raleigh, where he completed the Blandwood drawings and was introduced to the capital's society. William Haigh met Davis at a party on February 14, 1844: "Among the crowd was a Mr. Davis, an architect from New York, who is said to be a fine reader of Shakespeare, but [he] made an awful out at telling a tale, getting through with it long before the company had found the point and laughing part!"[19] In June, after Davis had returned to New York, Morehead asked Davis to buy pictures and frames for the new house. "I may trouble [you] to buy such things for me in the progress of my building," he wrote. "I shall be so busy this summer in politics & building that I shall not have much time to devote to matters of taste." That fall, when the Governor visited New York, Davis drove him 'round the picturesque reservoir at still pastoral 42nd Street, entertained him and helped with more household purchases.[20] Blandwood was illustrated by Davis in the second edition of Andrew Jackson Downing's *Treatise on the Theory and Practice of Landscape Gardening*, issued in 1844. Blandwood is open to the public.

Three years later, Robert Donaldson and his brother James hired Davis to design a Presbyterian Church at Chapel Hill. The plan, elevation and a perspective view were made between February 15 and 20, 1847.[21] More details were sent in May.[22] Davis felt that a Gothic design would be too expensive and that a spire alone would double the cost, so he selected what he called "Vitruvian Tuscan" as a practical style which would be appropriate for Protestant worship. The church was to be a small temple with Tuscan portico, columns in antis and strongly projecting, bracketed roof, loosely modelled on Inigo Jones's 17th-century St. Paul's, Covent Garden. In the dreary winter of 1848, after Davis had

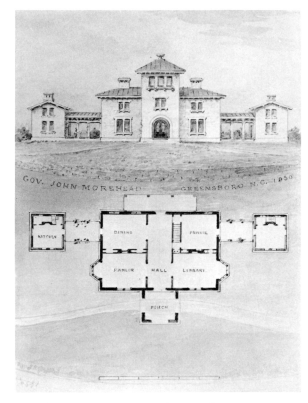

Blandwood, Greensboro, drawing by A. J. Davis. *Metropolitan Museum of Art, Harris Brisbane Dick Fund, 24.66.1405(119)*

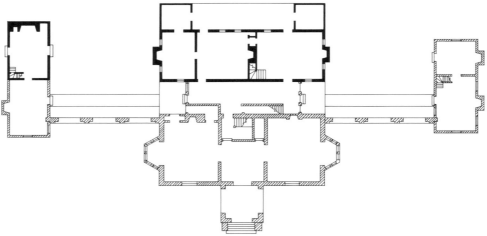

Blandwood, John Motley Morehead House, Greensboro, 1844, with a plan indicating
Davis's additions to the old house.

Top: Presbyterian Church, Chapel Hill, study by A. J. Davis, 1847. *Metropolitan Museum of Art, Harris Brisbane Dick Fund, 24.66.1233.* Bottom: Alumni Hall, University of North Carolina, Chapel Hill, study by A. J. Davis, 1850. *New-York Historical Society*

Presbyterian Church, Chapel Hill, 1847. *North Carolina Collection, University of North Carolina*

specified that the church should be painted "lilac grey," the church authorities begged clarification from the architect: "Now it has been so long since the last spring that our mason has forgotten the color of lilacs. ... Will you be pleased to help him & us?"[23] The church burned in 1919.

President Swain had the new Presbyterian Church in mind when, in 1849, he asked Davis to design a new assembly hall and library for the University.[24] Swain wanted another Tuscan temple like the church, but, though Davis made studies which included such a design, he finally declared that a small village like Chapel Hill should not have two important buildings so similar in style. In the spring of 1850, when Davis returned to North Carolina, the architect spent a week in mid-May with President Swain in Chapel Hill, where he conferred with the builder John Berry and enlarged the plan.[25] In Raleigh, on May 17, Davis had another "sitting over the plan for Alumni Hall, C. Hill."[26] And as soon as he returned to New York, Davis spent four days making revised drawings, which he mailed to Chapel Hill on May 31.[27] More than a year was spent experimenting with studies for various exterior treatments and alternate plans, including an "Elevation Hexastyle"[28] (a portico with six frontal columns) and Corinthian columns "from an example at Athens."[29] The building was to be stuccoed grey to simulate granite, and the capitals of the columns, carved in wood by Crane and Smith of New York, were to be decorated with corn cobs and wheat sheaves (tobacco was originally to be included but was then deleted)[30] in place of the acanthus leaves normally used for the Corinthian order. Davis described his ideas for the interior in 1850: "Great assembly room, lined with pilasters, 12 inches deep all around and 5 ft. wide for shelves. The intervals to be covered by a muslin curtain (painted with flowers) shewn at times of assembly, and at library hours to be rolled up like a window curtain. ... The ceiling I make nearly flat ... more in pure Greek style than the arch."[31] In 1925, when the hall was converted into a theater, Davis's interior was changed. The hall had a stone foundation, brick walls and tin roof.

Meanwhile, the North Carolina legislature had agreed to build a state Lunatic Asylum. In October, 1849, ex-Governor Morehead, chairman of the Asylum's building committee, visited Davis in New York. "Gov. M. with me all evening about asylum," Davis recorded in his journal.[32] At that meeting, Davis gave Morehead the published views of the Pauper Lunatic Asylum on Blackwell's Island, New York, which he had designed in the mid-1830's. It was a sprawling scheme with long wings, towers, wide, bracketed eaves, Davisean windows and Tuscan details. Davis would use this design as a model for both the new Asylum and

Corn-and-wheat capital, Alumni Hall, University of North Carolina, Chapel Hill

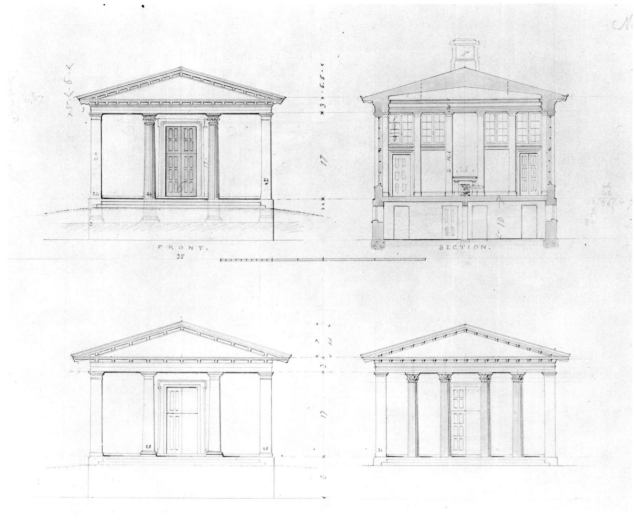

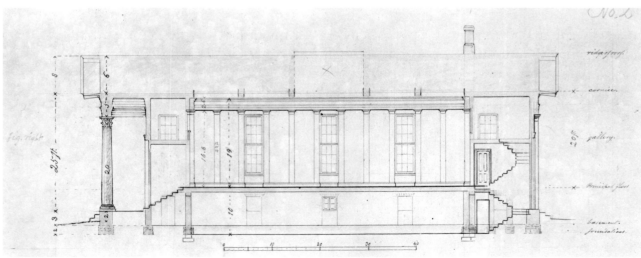

Alumni Hall, University of North Carolina, Chapel Hill, studies by A. J. Davis, 1850.
Metropolitan Museum of Art, Harris Brisbane Dick Fund, 24.66.1801 and 24.66.1799

Alumni Hall, 19th-century photographs. *North Carolina Collection,*
University of North Carolina

Davidson College, also in North Carolina. (In fact, Davis had modelled his Blackwell's Island building on the Middlesex Lunatic Hospital, London, designed by William Anderson and completed in May, 1831. Its plan consisted of a central tower with projections leading, at right angles, to extended wings. This building, though known as the County Asylum at Hanwell, still stands, just over the boundary at Southall.)

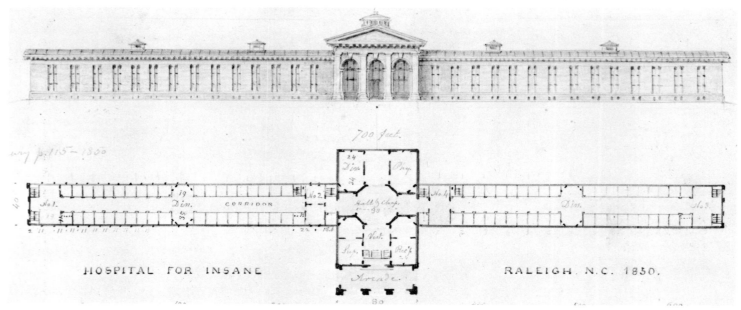

HOSPITAL FOR INSANE   RALEIGH. N.C. 1850.

Lunatic Asylum, Raleigh, drawing by A. J. Davis. *Metropolitan Museum of Art, Harris Brisbane Dick Fund, 24.66.1403(19)*

In December, 1849, Davis received the formal commission to design the North Carolina Asylum, and Morehead instructed the architect to visit "the crack and most recently constructed" mental hospitals of Providence, Hartford, Trenton, Philadelphia and Staunton, Virginia.[33] In April, 1850, Davis came to North Carolina by way of Trenton, Philadelphia and Staunton. Brick-making had already begun when Davis met the six members of the building committee on May 17. They surveyed the property and located the best site for the building.[34] Davis returned to New York at the end of the month and sent some ten drawings of the hospital to North Carolina in June and July, including a front elevation which was eight feet long.[35] (The most striking thing about the Asylum was its tremendous scale.) Dr. Francis R. Stribling, superintendent of the Western Asylum of Virginia, came to Raleigh and spent several days inspecting the site and suggesting many thoughtful alterations to Davis's plans.[36] In November, Davis returned to Raleigh and conferred again with the committee.[37] More drawings were produced until at least August, 1852.[38] By October, 1853, though the south wing was only two stories high, the brick walls of the central block and north wing had been completed. During the winter of 1854 window and

Lunatic Asylum, Raleigh, 1850–56. *Photograph by Wayne Andrews*

FOR Dr. WIER, GREENSBORO'N.CAROLINA.

DAVIS ARCT. 1844

A STUDY.

Drawing for Dr. David Weir House, Greensboro, and the plan, opposite, by A. J. Davis, 1844. *Metropolitan Museum of Art, Harris Brisbane Dick Fund, 24.66.1020 and 24.66.1021*

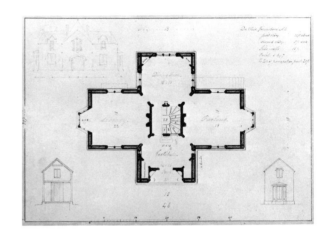

door frames were installed and floors were laid in the wings. In August, 1854, all walls were complete, the tin roof and copper gutters were being installed and separate kitchen and laundry buildings were under construction.[39] Equipped with steam heat, gas lighting, running water and a fresh-air ventilation system propelled by steam-powered fans, the hospital received its first patients in February, 1856. Most of the Asylum, which Davis himself praised as "a great work," has been demolished.

Robert Donaldson may have launched Davis's career in North Carolina, but it was Governor Morehead, a member of the building committees of the University and Asylum, who provided friendly introductions to possible clients for more than fifteen years. When Davis first visited Greensboro in 1844, he had met David Weir, an Irishman and friend of Morehead, and designed a house for him.[40] Had the house been built, it would have been one of North Carolina's most important and interesting. Davis's beautiful drawings show the architect's characteristic Romantic details—a commanding central gable, tall chimney stacks, stepped end gables, bay and oriel windows, Tudor arches, drip mouldings and casement windows. These elements were incorporated in two other famous Davis designs of the same era, the Delamater House, Rhinebeck, New York, 1843, and the Rotch House, New Bedford, Massachusetts, 1845. Curiously, while these two Northern residences had verandahs, the Weir House in hot North Carolina did not. Weir's house is noteworthy for its cruciform plan, central stair flanked by chimneys, and octagonal vestibule and octagonal dining room.

Another friend of Governor Morehead was Edwin M. Holt, a cotton mill owner, railroad director and farmer of Alamance County. Holt saw Morehead's copy of the January, 1849, issue of A. J. Downing's *Horticulturalist* magazine, with a frontispiece illustrating a small villa which had been designed by Davis for a client in Rahway, New Jersey. In March, Holt requested more details from Davis, who supplied designs which were executed, crudely, by a local builder, Eli Denny.[41]

Yet another friend of Governor Morehead was William A. Graham of Hillsborough, a lawyer, state legislator, senator, Governor from 1845 to 1849 and a member of the University's building committee. In the fall of 1850, Davis visited Montrose, Graham's home, an old Federal-style frame house.[42] During the first week of February, 1851, back in New York, Davis took the sketches made at Hillsborough and devised a plan for enlarging the house, adding new parlors with bay windows, dining room and octagonal library. He submitted two alternative exterior designs—one he described as "Old English," the other he described as "Italian."[43] But these plans were delayed while Graham was busy in

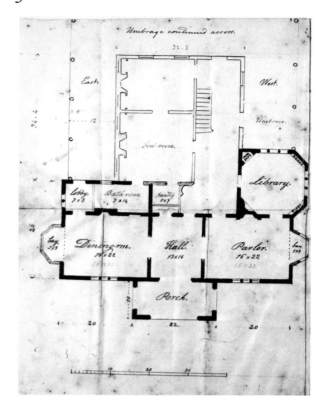

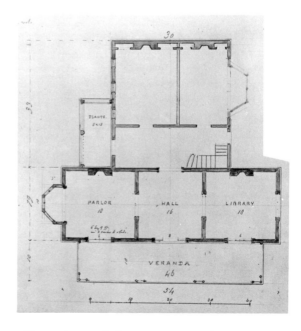

Top: Plan and alternate designs for additions to Montrose, William Graham House, Hillsborough vicinity, by A. J. Davis, 1851. *Private Collection.* Bottom: Plan and exterior design for additions to Jesse Lindsey House, Greensboro, by A. J. Davis, 1853. *New-York Historical Society*

Washington as Secretary of the Navy, and, finally, abandoned. In 1854 Graham wrote, apologetically, to Davis, explaining his change of plans and enclosing a check for $50.[44] The house at Montrose burned in 1862.

In 1844 Davis had met Jesse H. Lindsay, Morehead's brother-in-law, a University of North Carolina graduate, banker and state legislator, who also lived in Greensboro. In September, 1852, Robert Lindsay appeared at Davis's office in New York and asked the architect to design improvements to his brother's house. Taking a sketch which Robert Lindsay had carried with him from North Carolina, Davis "put into shape . . . and designed [an] elevation."[45] More drawings were sent in January, 1853.[46] From a surviving sketch, it appears that Davis proposed to add bay windows, new rooms, a conservatory, bracketed eaves, trellice-work verandah and a central gable to an older house.

Governor Morehead was also responsible for most of several commissions which came to Davis for institutional buildings. It is not known what became of plans prepared in July, 1851, for the Female College at Greensboro or the plans prepared in May, 1853, for Edgeworth Female Seminary at Greensboro.[47] The Female College, sponsored by the Methodists, had been built between 1843 and 1845, a three-story brick structure with thirty-six rooms. Wings were added, perhaps to Davis's design, in 1856 and 1859, but the building burned with all the college's records in 1863. Edgeworth Female Seminary had been established by Governor Morehead in 1839. The father of five daughters, Morehead purchased land next to his own home and paid for a four-story brick building, since destroyed. In October, 1853, Davis designed a new hall for Salem's Female Seminary, a boarding school operated by the Moravians since 1802. A four-story brick building, with a commanding Doric portico, was built between 1854 and 1856, but it is not known for certain if Davis's design was the one used. (An elevation drawing, without the portico, does not appear to have been drawn by Davis.) In June, 1857, Davis prepared drawings for a hotel for Governor Morehead and a preliminary design for a courthouse at Greensboro.[48] The hotel was not built, and the plans of another architect were used for the courthouse, which had been completed by April, 1860.[49]

Between July 23 and July 31, 1856, Davis made a final visit to Chapel Hill, where the University, now with some 360 students enrolled, was again outgrowing its buildings. In September, Davis sent drawings to President Swain. The architect proposed to enlarge Gerrard Hall, the old chapel, by extending its western end and adding a new portico and cupola. He proposed to improve the appearance of the old South Building, whose roof he considered too high and too steep, by adding a new

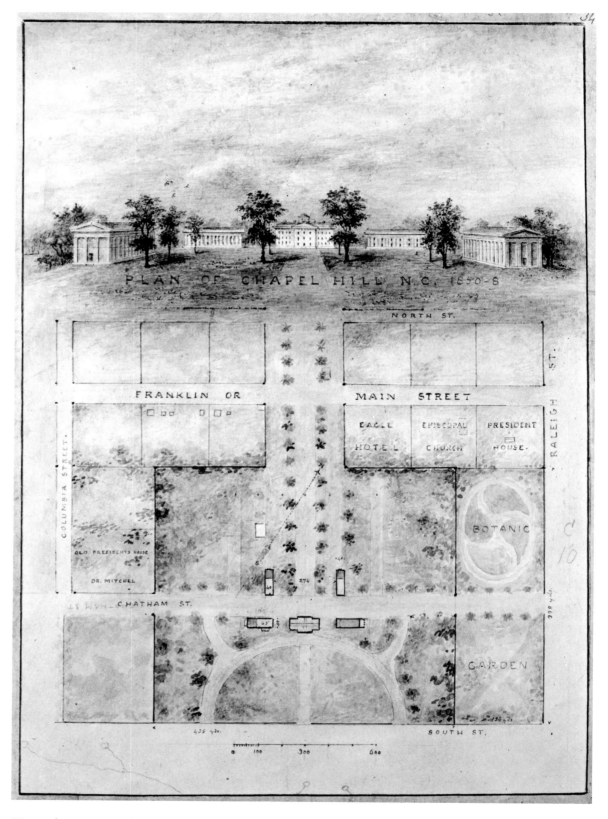

View of University of North Carolina, Chapel Hill, by A. J. Davis, c. 1856, showing his master plan for improvements. *Metropolitan Museum of Art, Harris Brisbane Dick Fund, 24.66.1406(30)*

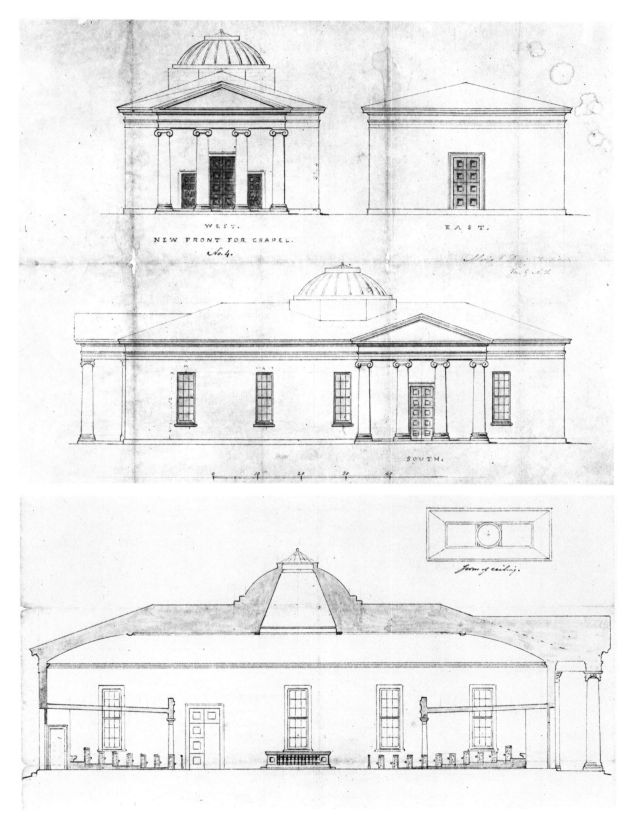

WEST.

NEW FRONT FOR CHAPEL.
No. 4.

EAST.

SOUTH.

Design for enlargement of Chapel, University of North Carolina, c. 1856, by A. J. Davis.
University Archives, University of North Carolina

cornice, portico and cupola.[50] These additions were intended to give further dignity and formality to the arrangement of the University's buildings. The enlarged chapel, with its new portico, would balance Smith Hall, with its portico, and the improved South Building, with its new cupola and portico, would be the centerpiece of the University. Davis prepared a beautiful drawing of his ideas for the new campus, with buildings he had designed in red ink and paths, promenades and gardens painted in shades of green. An admonition he had sent to President Swain a few years before would have still been useful: "Please observe that the road or path turnings and crooks in the sketch . . . are not capriciously made, but designed so as to present sunny and shady places for trees that flourish best in sun or shade."[51] But Swain had already warned Davis in June, 1856: "With the opulence of New York at our command we would find comparatively little difficulty in determining what ought to be and what might be done, but we are compelled to adjust our system of operations to the condition of things in North Carolina and an architect from the great city of the new world may find it difficult to limit his views to the narrow range of his resources."[52] Now Swain showed the drawings to the veteran builder John Berry, who warned that it would all be terribly expensive and, particularly, that the roof of the old chapel would not support a dome and extended walls. The University decided that money would be better spent on completely new buildings, and in 1858 William Percival, an architect with an office in Raleigh, was hired to design them.

After leaving Chapel Hill at the end of July, 1856, Davis travelled to Davidson College, twenty miles north of Charlotte, to meet with a committee planning new buildings.[53] Davidson College had opened in 1837 with scarcely one hundred students and a handful of rough brick buildings. When Maxwell Chambers, a wealthy Salisbury merchant, died in 1855, he left money for new college buildings. For Davis, this would be an opportunity for a bold, unified architectural vision, not the improvised and compromised, though creative, improvements which had occupied him at Chapel Hill. Davis began work in September and October, 1856. Detailed drawings were sent to Davidson between March, 1858, and June, 1859.[54] The cornerstone was laid in the spring of 1858. Bricks were made on the place, stone for the foundation and portico came from a quarry three miles away, and lime was dug near the banks of the Catawba River. Completed in January, 1860, the building contained seventy-two dormitory rooms, five classrooms, three laboratories, a large square assembly hall and library. It was destroyed by fire in November, 1921. Though five of Davis's detailed drawings survived

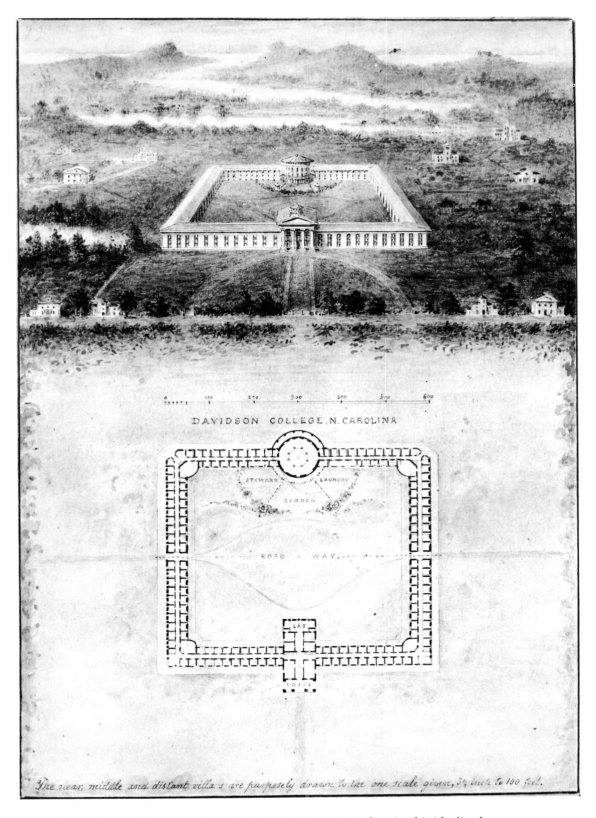

View of Davidson College, Davidson, by A. J. Davis, c. 1856, showing his idealized
plan for the academic and residential quadrangle. *Avery Library*

Davidson College, Davidson, 1858–60, 19th-century photograph. *Davidson College*

the fire, they were subsequently misplaced and are known only through photographs now at the University of North Carolina. Using a variation of his characteristic Davisean windows, the architect combined six windows on three floors, pairing those at the extreme corners of adjacent rooms and linking the pattern of windowpanes together with rectangular panels, to form what the viewer perceives as a single columnar shaft between flanking pilasters.

Davis's plan for Davidson College was related to his earlier design for the Pauper Lunatic Asylum on Blackwell's Island, New York, 1834, and the North Carolina Lunatic Asylum, 1850–56, both sprawling plans inspired by London's Middlesex Lunatic Hospital. The executed structure at Davidson, though monumental in composition and gigantic in scale, was only the central part of one building in an even grander plan for a collegiate quadrangle. Davis envisioned two U-shaped buildings, arranged to form a single enclosure. One building had a gable roof and pedimented portico, the other would have had a dome and semicircular colonnade. Together they would have contained academic halls, dining rooms, offices, chapel, kitchen and laundry. Davis's activities at Davidson were, of course, cut short by the coming of the Civil War.

Davis closed his office in 1878 and spent his remaining years arranging and rearranging his papers. In 1880, twelve years before his death in 1892, Davis wrote to Charles Phillips at Chapel Hill, asking what had become of his old friends in North Carolina and his final suggestions for the University's architecture. Phillips replied mournfully: "I well remember some of those suggestions. But . . . to keep alive, not to adorn, is the object . . . throughout the South. It is quite out of the question for the University of North Carolina to realize your great thoughts for it. . . . My heart fails me when I look on what is around me and think of what you said ought to be here. . . . The South is poor and lacking in hopefulness. . . . Vitruvius, Downing, &c. would meet with but deaf ears now!"[55]

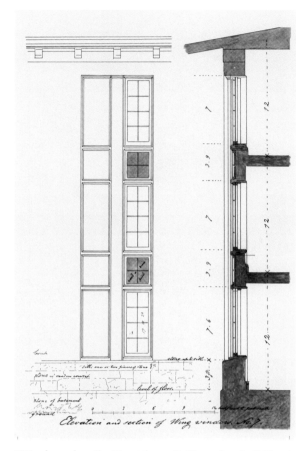

Window details, Davidson College, by A. J. Davis, c. 1859, redrawn from photocopy of lost original.

Notes

Every student of North Carolina architecture is indebted to Thomas Tileston Waterman for his pioneering *Early Architecture of North Carolina* (Chapel Hill, 1941), though two generations of research over the last forty years, inspired by his work, have superseded most of his information. The following notes indicate, in place of a separate bibliography, useful manuscript and published information about North Carolina and its historic architecture. The notes also thank several local experts for their guidance and encouragement. Without the help of these works and generous friends a book like *Architecture of the Old South* would be quite impossible.

I. THE COLONY

1. Richard Hakluyt, *A discourse Concerning Western Planting* (orig. 1584, reprinted Cambridge, 1877), pp. 164–165.

2. J. C. Harrington, "The Manufacture and Use of Bricks at the Raleigh Settlement on Roanoke Island," *North Carolina Historical Review* (*NCHR*), XLIV (1967), p. 1.

3. *Ibid.*, pp. 1–17.

4. Francis Yardley to John Farrar, May 8, 1654, in William L. Saunders, *The Colonial Records of North Carolina* (*CRNC*), I (1886), p. 18.

5. Carl Lounsbury, "Development of Domestic Architecture in the Albemarle Region," *NCHR*, LIV (1977), p. 20.

6. Hugh T. Lefler and William S. Powell, *Colonial North Carolina* (New York, 1973), p. 42.

7. Quoted in Wilson Angley, "A History of St. Thomas Episcopal Church, Bath, North Carolina," typescript, N. C. Division of Archives and History, 1981.

8. Earl Gregg Swem, ed., *An Account of the Cape Fear Country* (Perth Amboy, 1922), p. 15.

9. This is the first of several references from the comprehensive research files at the Museum of Early Southern Decorative Arts, Winston-Salem.

10. John Lawson, *A New Voyage to Carolina* (Chapel Hill, 1967), pp. 100, 107.

11. *CRNC*, VII, pp. 201–202.

12. The author is indebted to A. L. Hunnicutt of the N.C. Department of Cultural Resources for his guidance on the history of Newbold-White House. Thomas C. Parramore, "The Newbold-White House: A Documentary History of the Property and Its Inhabitants," typescript, N.C. Division of Archives and History, 1973.

13. Bruce S. Cheeseman, "The Cupola House of Edenton, Chowan County," typescript, N.C. Division of Archives and History, 1980.

14. John Brickell, *The Natural History of North-Carolina* (Dublin, 1743), p. 37.

15. Jerry L. Cross, "The Palmer-Marsh House, Bath, North Carolina," typescript, N.C. Division of Archives and History, n.d.

16. Thomas T. Waterman, *The Dwellings of Colonial America* (Chapel Hill, 1950), p. 4.

17. *CRNC*, I, p. 559.

18. *Ibid.*, p. 710.

19. *Ibid.*, p. 684.

20. Quoted in Wilson Angley, *op. cit.*

21. Wilson Angley's typescript research report. *op. cit.*, provides the history of St. Thomas and early churches in North Carolina.

22. *CRNC*, VII, p. 164.

23. *CRNC*, V, p. 595.

24. *Ibid.*, pp. 597–599.

25. Louis B. Wright and Marion Tinling, *Quebec to Carolina* (San Marino, 1943), pp. 266, 275, 287.

26. David Sutton Phelps, "An Archaeological Study of the King-Bazemore House, Bertie County, North Carolina," typescript East Carolina University, 1980. Anastasia Sims, "The King House of Bertie County," typescript N.C. Division of Archives and History, 1976.

27. Inventory of John Hawks, March 10, 1791, Craven County, Estate Papers, N.C. Archives, Raleigh.

28. William S. Powell, *The Correspondence of William Tryon and Other Selected Papers* (Raleigh, 1980), II, p. 400. Alonzo Thomas Dill, Jr., "Tryon's Palace," *NCHR*, XIX, (1942), pp. 119–167. Fiske Kimball and Gertrude S. Carraway, "Tryon's Palace," New-York Historical Society *Quarterly Bulletin*, 24 (1940), pp. 13–20. Alonzo Thomas Dill, *Governor Tryon and His Palace* (Chapel Hill, 1955).

29. *CRNC*, VII, p. 431. The original ms. is in the Gratz Collection, Historical Society of Pennsylvania.

30. *CRNC*, VIII, p. 7. William S. Powell, *op. cit.*, II, p. 289.

31. *CRNC*, VIII, p. 285.

32. Lida Tunstall Rodman, "Journal of a Tour of North Carolina by William Attmore, 1787," *James Sprunt Historical Publications*, 17 (Chapel Hill, 1922).

33. Builder's estimate, in Powell, *op. cit.*, I, pp. 610–611.

34. Hugh Buckner Johnston, "The Journal of Ebenezer Hazzard in North Carolina," *NCHR*, XXXVI, (1959), p. 375.

35. *CRNC*, VIII, p. 8.

36. Powell, *op. cit.*, II, p. 289.

37. Walter Clark, *The State Records of North Carolina*, XXII (Goldboro, 1907), p. 961.

38. Joseph A. Hoskins, *President Washington's Diaries* (Summerfield, N.J., 1921), p. 21.

39. *North Carolina Gazette*, New Bern, June 4, 1791, July 26, 1794.

40. *Virginia Gazette*, Williamsburg, June 4, 1767.

41. John Hawks to Joseph Hewes, September 29,

1773, John Hawks Papers, Southern Historical Collection, University of North Carolina (UNC).

42. *Virginia Gazette*, Williamsburg, February 4, 1768.

43. Church contract is at Archives of the Episcopal Church, Austin, Texas.

44. "The Burgwin-Wright House," Lower Cape Fear Historical Society *Bulletin*, XXII (1979), pp. 1, 4.

45. "Preliminary Report on the John Wright Stanly House, New Bern, North Carolina," typescript, Tryon Palace Commission, 1966.

II. ACROSS THE FRONTIER

1. *CRNC*, IV, p. 1312.
2. *CRNC*, VII, p. 248.
3. *Ibid.*, p. 101.
4. *Ibid.*, p. 288.
5. "Biographical Sketch of Waightstill Avery with Illustrative Manuscripts," *North-Carolina University Magazine*, IV, (1885).
6. John Lawson, *A New Voyage to Carolina* (Chapel Hill, 1967), pp. 223–224.
7. Louis B. Wright, *The Prose Works of William Byrd of Westover* (Cambridge, 1966), pp. 206–207.
8. Elizabeth A. Fennt and Peter H. Wood, *Natives and Newcomers* (Chapel Hill, 1983), p. 31.
9. Adelaide L. Fries, *Records of the Moravian Church in North Carolina (RMCNC)*, I (Raleigh, 1922), p. 96.
10. *CRNC*, V, p. 355.
11. *Ibid.*, p. 362.
12. *Ibid.*, p. 476.
13. Jerry Clyde Cashion, "Fort Dobbs," typescript, N.C. Division of Archives and History, 1968.
14. *CRNC*, V, p. 849.
15. *RMCNC*, I, pp. 73–74.
16. *Ibid.*, p. 268.
17. *RMCNC*, II, p. 531.
18. *RMCNC*, V, p. 2147.
19. *Ibid.*, p. 2142.
20. "Memoir of Friedrich Wilhelm von Marschall," typescript, Moravian Archives of the Southern Province, Winston-Salem.
21. Betty Jean Campbell, "The Buildings of Salem, North Carolina, 1766–1856," Ph.D. thesis, Florida State University, 1975. Old Salem, Inc. has accumulated comprehensive research files on each historic site in Salem, which supplement the published Moravian records for the chronology in this chapter.
22. Building Code, Moravian Archives.
23. Elders Conference, July 23, 1771, Moravian Archives.
24. Frederick Marshall's comments about timber-frame construction are found in *RMCNC*, I, p. 315.
25. Johann Ettwein to Vorsteher Collegium, 1766, Moravian Archives.
26. Helpers Conference, June 6, 1766, Moravian Archives.
27. Matthew Schropp to Br. Seidel, October 5, 1766, Moravian Archives.
28. *RMCNC*, II, p. 604.
29. Helpers Conference, November 6, 1769, Moravian Archives.
30. Frank L. Horton, "Bethabara Church and Gemeinhaus, typescript, Winston-Salem, 1970.
31. *RMCNC*, V, p. 2045.
32. *Ibid.*, p. 2339.
33. Frank P. Albright, *The Home Moravian Church* (Winston-Salem, 1983).
34. *RMCNC*, VI, p. 2627.
35. Reichel to Loskiel, May 25, 1804–05, Moravian Archives.
36. L. Newby ltr., August 18, 1823, Moravian Archives.
37. *RMCNC*, V, p. 2096.
38. Adam Spach's autobiography is included in Henry Wesley Foltz, *Descendants of Adam Spach* (Raleigh, 1924).
39. Richard M. Iobst, "Preliminary Report on the Hezekiah Alexander House," typescript, N.C. Division of Archives and History, 1969.
40. Maurice C. York, "The Many Faces of Fort Defiance," typescript, N.C. Division of Archives and History, 1969.
41. Stephen E. Massengill, "The House in the Horseshoe," typescript, N.C. Division of Archives and History, 1973.
42. A. R. Newsome, "Twelve North Carolina Counties in 1810–1811," *NCHR*, V, (1928), pp. 423–424, 440, and VI (1929), pp. 285, 299, 306.
43. Louis B. Wright and Marion Tinling, *Quebec to Carolina* (San Marino, 1943), p. 275.
44. Bernard Duke of Saxe-Weimar Eisenach, *Travels Through North America* (Philadelphia, 1828).
45. C. D. Arfwedson, *The United States and Canada* (London, 1834), I, p. 362.
46. *Compendium of the Enumeration of the Inhabitants and Statistics of the United States* (Washington, 1841), p. 185.
47. *NCHR*, XXXIII (1956), p. 391.
48. *Southern Weekly Post*, Raleigh, October 15, 1853.

III. THE FEDERAL ERA

1. J. H. Smith to Duncan Cameron, March 10, 1829, Cameron Family Papers, Southern Historical Collection, UNC.
2. *Wilmington Gazette*, April 28, 1803.
3. Builder's contract, March 8, 1799, John Steele Papers, Southern Historical Collection, UNC.
4. Memorandum of agreement between John Steele

and John Langdon, John Steele Papers, Southern Historical Collection, UNC.

5. James H. Craig, *The Arts and Crafts in North Carolina, 1699–1840* (Winston-Salem, 1965), p. 165.

6. William R. Davie to John Steele, August 3, 1801, quoted in Davyd Foard Hood, *The Architecture of Rowan County* (Salisbury, 1983).

7. James H. Craig's *The Arts and Crafts in North Carolina* is a useful documentary record. The forthcoming publication of *Architects and Builders of North Carolina*, by Catherine Bishir, Charlotte V. Brown and Carl Lounsbury, with research by Marshall Bullock and William R. Bushung, will be vital.

8. *The Star and North Carolina State Gazette*, Raleigh, October 11, 1816.

9. *The Raleigh Minerva*, September 27, 1810.

10. *North-Carolina Chronicle*, Fayetteville, September 27, 1790. *The Edenton Gazette*, March 2, 1808.

11. Frank Horton and John Bivins, "Restoration of the John Haley House," typescript, 1969, at High Point Museum.

12. *Raleigh Star*, August 19, 1814.

13. Specifications for the State House, c. 1792, in Cameron Family Papers, Southern Historical Collection, UNC.

14. *Fayetteville Gazette*, August 6, 1793.

15. *North-Carolina Gazette*, New Bern, February 24, 1798.

16. *Raleigh Star*, November 15, 1810.

17. Appearance of campus suggested by contract dated March 3, 1795, University Papers, UNC.

18. James Patterson to John Haywood, August 18, 1795, University Papers, UNC.

19. Specifications for the President's House, January 25, 1794, University Papers, UNC.

20. Jean B. Anderson, "A Preliminary Report on Stagville Plantation," typescript, N.C. Division of Archives and History, 1977.

21. The author is indebted to John Tyler of Roxobel, North Carolina, for information and help.

22. Norman D. Askins, "Architectural Report: Semple House," typescript, Colonial Williamsburg Foundation, 1971–72, suggests Halfpenny as a source.

23. James G. Burr, *The Hermitage* (Wilmington, 1855).

24. Eliza Clitherall Reminiscences, Volume 2, C. P. E. Burgwin Collection, Southern Historical Collection, UNC.

25. John R. Donnell Account Book, September 15, 1818, Bryan Papers, Southern Historical Collection, UNC.

26. Lynda Vestal Herzog, "The Early Architecture of New Bern, North Carolina, 1750–1850," Ph.D. thesis, University of California, Los Angeles, 1977.

27. *Edenton Intelligencer*, June 4, 1788.

28. *Carolina Centinel*, New Bern, October 16, 1819.

29. *The Raleigh Minerva*, April 9, 1819.

30. James Torrence Daybook, pp. 109, 111, private collection.

31. Cameron Family Papers, Southern Historical Collection, UNC.

32. Catherine Bishir, "The Montmorenci-Prospect Hill School" in Doug Swaim, *Carolina Dwelling* (Raleigh, 1978), pp. 84–103.

33. C. Ford Peatross, *William Nichols Architect* (n.p., 1979).

34. Inventory titled "Negroes at Hayes, March, 1814," in Hayes Collection, Southern Historical Collection. UNC.

35. Receipt for bricks from James Cunningham, March, 1815; James Johnston to William Wilkins, June 14, 1815; Memorandum, August 16, 1815, all in Hayes Collection.

36. Marshall Parks to James Johnston, September 1, 1815, Hayes Collection.

37. William Nichols to James Johnston, May 1, 1817, Hayes Collection.

38. James Johnston to Joseph Blount, July 15, 1817, Hayes Collection.

39. James Johnston to Joseph Blount, November 9, 1817, Hayes Collection.

40. State House, Materials and Supplies for Renovations, 1821, N.C. Archives, Raleigh.

41. *Raleigh Register*, October 19, 1821.

42. The author is indebted to Edgar Thorne of Inez, North Carolina, for help given and troubles endured to gather information about these temple-like houses in his area.

43. Michael R. Hill, "Historical Research Report, The Person Place of Louisburg, North Carolina," typescript, N.C. Division of Archives and History, 1980.

IV. THE GREEK REVIVAL

1. Daybook, p. 298, A. J. Davis Collection, New York Public Library (NYPL).

2. Jean B. Anderson, "Fairntosh Plantation and the Camerons," typescript, North Carolina Division of Archives and History, 1978.

3. *Niles Register*, July 2, 1831, p. 310.

4. William Strickland to the Commissioners, November 10, 1837, Paton Papers, N.C. Archives, Raleigh. Strickland objected to a balustrade proposed by Paton to surround the dome. "A balustrade," he wrote, "is Roman and inadmissable!"

5. *Star*, Raleigh, April 3, 1839.

6. Daybook, pp. 125, 143, A. J. Davis Collection, NYPL.

7. Diary, p. 18, Davis Collection, Metropolitan Museum of Art, New York.

8. Daybook, p. 149, A. J. Davis Collection, NYPL.

9. William Gaston to Susan Jane Donaldson, February 24, 1833, William Gaston Papers, Southern Historical Collection, UNC.

10. *Star*, Raleigh, March 1, 1833, and March 5, 1833.

11. *Raleigh Register*, April 9, 1833.

12. *Ibid.*, January 13, 1833.

13. *Observer*, Fayetteville, January 15, 1833; *Raleigh Register*, January 18, 1833.

14. Ithiel Town to David Paton, March 2, 1835, Paton Papers, N.C. Archives, Raleigh.

15. *Star*, Raleigh, August 14, 1834; *Raleigh Register*, August 12, 1834.

16. A. J. Davis witnessed the agreement between Town and Paton, in the Paton Papers, N.C. Archives. *The Memorial of David Paton* (Edinburgh, 1843). Stephen N. Dennis and John L. Sanders, "David Paton, Architect," typescript, Institute of Government, Chapel Hill, 1972. The author is indebted to Mr. Sanders for help and encouragement.

17. Board of Commissioners to William W. Barth, March 31, 1835, D. J. Harrill Collection, N.C. Archives.

18. Town to Paton, March 2, 1835, Paton Papers, N.C. Archives.

19. Robert Mills to David Paton, February 16, 1836, Paton Papers, N.C. Archives.

20. Commissioners to William Strickland, October 30, 1837. In March, 1841, Strickland asked to be paid $150 for past "advice and assistance in revising and consulting with their Architect Mr. Paton." William Strickland to S. Birdsall, March 10, 1841, in Treasurers' and Comptrollers' Papers, State Capitol, Construction Architect Fees, 1834–41, N.C. Archives.

21. The progress of construction is outlined in several reports to the legislature, in manuscript and pamphlets in N.C. Archives.

22. *Hillsborough Recorder*, April 4, 1838.

23. *Hillsborough Recorder*, June 2, 1837.

24. Report of David Paton, February 13, 1840, in Treasurers' and Comptrollers' Papers, N.C. Archives.

25. *Star*, Raleigh, June 17, 1840.

26. W. McPheeters to David Paton, December 21, 1835, Paton Papers, N.C. Archives.

27. *Chronicle*, Wilmington, October 1, 1845.

28. Robert Mills to the Secretary of the Treasury, March 21, 1843; Edward B. Dudley and others to President John Tyler, September 16, 1843; Murphy V. Jones to the Secretary of the Treasury, February 15, 1845, and February 20, 1845; Robert B. Wood to the Secretary of the Treasury, November 1, 1848; all in Treasury Secretary's Office, Letters Received Relating to the Construction of Custom Houses and Other Structures, National Archives.

29. *Wilmington Journal*, August 22, 1845, quoted in Mary Lane Morrison, *John S. Norris* (Savannah, 1980), pp. 56–57.

30. *Hillsborough Recorder*, September 12, 1844.

31. C. Wingate Reed, *Beaufort County* (Raleigh, 1962), p. xx.

32. Davis records in his Diary, October 29–31, 1853, that he made a "Design for Francis Fries, Salem, North Carolina, 2 elevations for a female Seminary, 4 stories high," Avery Library, Columbia University, New York.

33. A. J. Downing, *Rural Essays* (New York, 1853), pp. 206–207, 246.

34. Anthony Trollope, *North America* (New York, 1951), p. 167.

35. Catherine Bishir, "Asher Benjamin's Practical House Carpenter in North Carolina," *Carolina Comments*, XXVII (1979), pp. 66–74.

36. Lola Carr Steelman, "The Life-Style of an Eastern North Carolina Planter," *NCHR*, LVIII (1980), pp. 17–42.

32. A contemporary description of Main Hall, from *The People's Press* of March 7, 1856, is quoted in Frances Griffin, *Less Time for Meddling: A History of Salem Academy and College* (Winston-Salem, 1979), pp. 246–247. Davis records in his Diary, October 29–31, 1853, that he made a "Design for Francis Fries, Salem, North Carolina, 2 elevations for a Female Seminary, 4 stories high," Avery Library, Columbia University, New York.

V. ROMANTIC STYLES

1. Charles Clinton Weaver, *Internal Improvements in North Carolina Previous to 1860* (Baltimore, 1903), collects several reports on internal improvements made to the state legislature.

2. *Annual Report of the Board of Public Improvements* (Raleigh, 1820).

3. *American Beacon and Commercial Directory*, Norfolk, August 29, 1816.

4. *American Beacon and Norfolk and Portsmouth Daily Advertiser*, Norfolk, November 6, 1818.

5. *Report of the Board of Internal Improvements* (Raleigh, 1833).

6. *Observer*, Fayetteville, August 24, 1831.

7. *Hillsborough Recorder*, May 19, 1837.

8. *Population of the United States in 1860* (Washington, 1864), pp. 362–363.

9. James Marshall Bullock, "The Enterprising Contractor, Mr. Cosby," M.A. thesis, University of North Carolina, 1982.

10. Dabney Cosby ltr., undated but c. 1844, Cosby Papers, Southern Historical Collection, UNC.

11. Eva Ingersoll Gatling, "John Berry of Hillsboro, North Carolina," *Journal of the Society of Architec-*

tural Historians, X (1951), pp. 18–22.

12. John Berry to Thomas Ruffin, June, 1831, Ruffin Papers, Southern Historical Collection, UNC.

13. Catherine W. Bishir, "Jacob W. Holt: An American Builder," *Winterthur Portfolio*, 16 (1981), pp. 1–31.

14. Obituary in *Wilmington Messenger*, July 16, 1899.

15. Advertisement for contractor for St. John's in *The Carolina Federal Republican*, New Bern, May 3, 1817.

16. Stephen D. Tyng, *Memoir of the Rev. Gregory T. Beddell* (Philadelphia, 1836).

17. John Henry Hopkins, *Essay on Gothic Architecture* (Burlington, 1832), pp. iv, 1, 2.

18. Church is described in *New York Ecclesiologist*, January, 1849. I am indebted to Philip A. Rees of Chapel Hill for guidance and for the useful information in his excellent "Chapel of the Cross, An Architectural History," M.A. thesis, University of North Carolina, 1979.

19. David Swain to Robert Donaldson, November 28, 1843, Swain Papers, Southern Historical Collection, UNC. Swain wrote, "The Episcopalians have erected the wall of a very neat church planned by Mr. Walter of Philadelphia."

20. Bishop L. S. Ives to Richard Upjohn, January 12 and 28, 1846, Upjohn Collection, NYPL.

21. R. S. Mason to Richard Upjohn, November 15, 1847, Upjohn Collection, NYPL.

22. R. S. Mason to Richard Upjohn, November 27, 1847, Upjohn Collection, NYPL.

23. *Ibid.*

24. John H. Parker to Richard Upjohn, November 16, 1849, Upjohn Collection, NYPL.

25. Lawrence Wodehouse, "Upjohn's 'Rural Architecture' in North Carolina," *North Carolina Architect*, 15 (1968), pp. 13–22.

26. Francis W. Hilliard to Richard Upjohn, April 12, 1859, Upjohn Collection, NYPL.

27. J. D. Hufnan, *Memoir of the Rev. John L. Pritchard* (Raleigh, 1867), pp. 112, 117, 121, 122, 125.

28. *NCHR*, XXXIII (1956), p. 407.

29. James Johnston to Bryan and Maitland, February 19, 1839, Hayes Collection, Southern Historical Collection, UNC.

30. Raymond L. Beck, "The Restoration of the Cabinet and Minerals Room in the State Capitol Building, Raleigh," typescript, 1977.

31. *Address Delivered on the Occasion of Laying the Corner Stone of the North Carolina Institution for the Instruction of the Deaf and Blind* (New York, 1848).

32. *Acts and Documents of the General Assembly and Reports of the Board of Directors of the North Carolina Institution for the Education of the Deaf, Blind and Dumb* (Raleigh, 1853).

33. Peter W. Hairston, "J. E. B. Stuart's Letters to His Hairston Kin, 1850–1055," *NCHR*, LI (1974), p. 314.

34. Harold N. Cooledge, Jr., "A Sloan Check List, 1849–1884," in *Journal of the Society of Architectural Historians*, XIX (1960), pp. 34–38. The author is indebted to Professor Cooledge for additional material from his forthcoming biography of Sloan.

35. Isabel M. Williams, "Thalian Hall," typescript, North Carolina Division of Archives and History, 1976.

36. William B. Bushong, "William Percival, An English Architect in the Old North State, 1857–1860," *NCHR*, LVII (1980), pp. 310–339.

37. Advertisement in *Southerner*, Tarboro, March 12, 1859.

38. *Iredell Express*, Statesville, January 7, 1859.

39. "List of Works designed and executed by me, E. G. Lind, since commencing business in Baltimore, Maryland, in the year 1856," Maryland Historical Society.

40. Obituary in American Institute of Architects *Quarterly Bulletin*, X (1909), pp. 130–131.

41. William B. Bushong, "An Architectural Oddity Down East, or the Octagon House of Hyde County," typescript, North Carolina Division of Archives and History.

42. The author is indebted to Leroy Wilson of Lexington, North Carolina, for information about the Sowers House.

43. Beverly Heisner, "Harriet Morrison Irwin's Hexagonal House," *NCHR*, LVIII (1981), pp. 105–123.

VI. A. J. DAVIS IN NORTH CAROLINA

1. Robert Donaldson to David Swain, November 10 and December 12, 1843, Swain Collection, Southern Historical Collection, UNC. For literary purposes, the author has mixed sentences from both letters.

2. John V. Allcott, "Architect A. J. Davis in North Carolina," *North Carolina Architect*, XX (1973), pp. 10–15. The author is indebted to Professor Allcott and to Mrs. Jane Davies of New York for selfless help and encouragement.

3. Advertisement clipping dated January, 1848, in Volume IV (Folio R) of A. J. Davis Collection, Metropolitan Museum.

4. John V. Allcott, "Robert Donaldson, the First North Carolinian to Become Prominent in the Arts," *NCHR*, LII (1975), pp. 333–366.

5. Daybook, p. 123, A. J. Davis Collection, NYPL.

6. Daybook, p. 141, Davis Collection, NYPL. Journal, p. 32, Davis Collection, Metropolitan Museum Philanthropic Society, "Estimate and Description of the Doric building," 1832, University Papers, UNC.

7. Journal, p. 41, Davis Collection, Metropolitan Museum.

8. Daybook, p. 273, Davis Collection, NYPL.

9. David Swain to Daniel L. Barringer, March 6, 1840, Swain Papers, Southern Historical Collection, UNC.

10. Robert Donaldson to A. J. Davis, January 14, 1844, Davis Collection, NYPL.

11. Journal, p. 75, Davis Collection, Metropolitan Museum.

12. Daybook, p. 253, Davis Collection, NYPL.

13. *Ibid.*, p. 271.

14. *Ibid.*, p. 343.

15. A. J. Davis to David Swain, March 24, 1845, Swain Papers, Southern Historical Collection, UNC.

16. Swain to Davis, December 20, 1844, Davis Collection, NYPL, reports preparations for construction.

17. Journal, p. 75, Davis Collection, Metropolitan Museum Daybook, p. 255, Davis Collection, NYPL.

18. Jane B. Davies, "Blandwood and the Italian Villa Style in America," *Nineteenth Century*, I (1975), pp. 11–14. Mary L. R. Edmunds, "Nineteenth Century Blandwood in North Carolina," *op. cit.*, pp. 6–10.

19. Diary, February 15, 1844, William Hooper Haigh Papers, quoted in William Bushong, "History of Blandwood," typescript, Greensboro Preservation Society, 1974.

20. Daybook, pp. 257, 267, Davis Collection, NYPL.

21. *Ibid.*, p. 339. Journal, p. 93, Davis Collection, Metropolitan Museum.

22. Daybook, p. 343, Davis Collection, NYPL.

23. Charles Phillips to A. J. Davis, March 3, 1848, Davis Collection, Avery Library, Columbia University.

24. John V. Allcott, "Scholarly Books and Frolicksome Blades," *Journal of the Society of Architectural Historians*, X (1974), pp. 145–154.

25. Journal, p. 114, Davis Collection, Metropolitan Museum.

26. Daybook, p. 407, Davis Collection, NYPL.

27. Journal, p. 114, Davis Collection, Metropolitan Museum. Daybook, p. 409, Davis Collection, NYPL.

28. Daybook, p. 399, Davis Collection, NYPL.

29. A. J. Davis to David Swain, March 4, 1850, quoted in Henderson, *The Campus of the First State University* (Chapel Hill, 1949), p. 139–141.

30. Henderson, *op. cit.*, p. 142. A. J. Davis to David Swain, May 31, 1850, Swain papers, Southern Historical Collection, UNC.

31. A. J. Davis to David Swain, March 4, 1850, Swain Papers, Southern Historical Collection, UNC.

32. Daybook, p. 391. Davis Collection, NYPL.

33. *Ibid.*, p. 393. J. M. Morehead to A. J. Davis, December 16, 1849, Davis Collection, NYPL.

34. Daybook, pp. 405–407, Davis Collection, NYPL. Journal, p. 115, Davis Collection, Metropolitan Museum.

35. Daybook, pp. 409–411, Davis Collection, NYPL.

36. Francis T. Stribling to A. J. Davis, August 2, 1850, Davis Collection, NYPL. *Report of the Commissioners of the Insane Hospital* (Raleigh, 1851).

37. Daybook, p. 419, Davis Collection, NYPL.

38. *Ibid.*, pp. 427, 447, 455.

39. *Report of Superintendent of the Lunatic Asylum* (Raleigh, 1854).

40. Journal, p. 75, Davis Collection, Metropolitan Museum.

41. Diary, Edwin Michael Holt Papers, Southern Historical Collection, UNC.

42. John V. Allcott, "Architectural Developments at Montrose in the 1850's," *NCHR*, XLII (1965), pp. 85–95.

43. Daybook, p. 423, Davis Collection, NYPL.

44. William Graham to A. J. Davis, July 3, 1854, Davis Collection, NYPL.

45. Daybook, p. 457, Davis Collection, NYPL. There is a sketch, dated September 20, 1852, of this house in Box 2, file 21, of the NYPL's Davis Collection.

46. A drawing at the New-York Historical Society is marked "For Jesse Lindsey, Esq., Greensboro, N.C., January, 1853."

47. Edgeworth drawings are listed in Journal, p. 147, Davis Collection, Metropolitan Museum. On May 23, 1853, in Daybook at the NYPL, Davis records "Edgeworth, Greensboro', plan, elevation, front, rear, end on yellow paper." NYPL has a drawing in Box 2, file 21.

48. Journal, p. 185, Davis Collection, Metropolitan Museum. The hotel and courthouse are both mentioned in another Journal at Columbia's Avery Library, p. 98. Jesse Lindsey to Davis, June 13, 1857, Davis Collection, Metropolitan Museum.

49. Lindsey to Davis, April 25, 1860, Davis Collection, Metropolitan Museum. Lindsey writes: "No part of your design was adopted. The Courthouse is now completed and in use."

50. Journal, p. 177, Davis Collection, Metropolitan Museum. Journal, p. 72, Davis Collection, Avery Library.

51. A. J. Davis to David Swain, March 9, 1847, Swain Papers, Southern Historical Collection, UNC.

52. D. L. Swain to A. J. Davis, June 18, 1856, Davis Collection, NYPL.

53. Journal, p. 178, Davis Collection, Metropolitan Museum. Journal p. 72, Davis Collection, Avery Library.

54. See Journal, pp. 112, 116, 146, Davis Collection, Avery Library.

55. Charles Phillips to A. J. Davis, November 29, 1880, Davis Collection, Avery Library.

Index